W9-BZJ-334

Managing Conflict

Managing Conflict: Tactics for School Administrators

RICHARD E. MAURER

Principal, Anne M. Dorner Middle School, Ossining, New York

Allyn and Bacon
Boston   London   Toronto   Sydney   Tokyo   Singapore

Library of Congress Cataloging-in-Publication Data

Maurer, Richard E.
    Managing conflict : tactics for school administrators. / Richard
E. Maurer.
        p.   cm.
    Includes bibliographical references.
    ISBN 0-205-12668-5
    1. School management and organization—Handbooks, manuals, etc.
2. Conflict management—Handbooks, manuals, etc.   I. Title.
LB2806.M373   1991
371.2—dc20   90-36330
                                                                            CIP

Printed in the United States of America
10 9 8 7 6 5 4 3 2 1 94 93 92 91 90

*For my parents, and Jeannette, Regina,
and especially Elizabeth*

Contents

CHAPTER THREE

Dealing with Demands, Anger, and Threats   73

CHAPTER FOUR

Resolving Conflict 109

CHAPTER FIVE

Getting What You Want 145

Introduction

- Your secretary informs you that there are two angry parents outside your office demanding to speak to you.

- At a board of education meeting, a group of community representatives presents you with a list of demands and calls for your resignation.

- The teachers' union president is threatening to call for a work slowdown unless the grievances presented to you are dealt with honorably.

A school administrator cannot avoid dealing with conflict. Hardly a day goes by that the school administrator is not either involved in a conflict or mediating one. Whether the demands come from your superiors, from various constituents in the community, from parents, from students, or from teaching staff, you, as the school administrator, are the one first called on to help resolve the conflict. This role of the school administrator in resolving conflict is one that demands extraordinary interpersonal skills as well as an ability to think critically and creatively.

This book is for administrators who want to learn how to deal more successfully with conflict. In this book you will learn more about the nature of conflict, become more aware of the conflict resolution skills you already possess, and learn how to implement additional skills that will help you bring conflict situations to successful resolutions.

The term *conflict* is used broadly in this book to refer to a disagreement between two or more individuals or groups over an issue or issues. This process of disagreement can be either formal or informal. In a *formal* conflict, the parties involved have specifically stated their disagreements about an issue. An *informal* conflict occurs when there is disagreement over an issue but neither party has yet explicitly communicated its position to the other.

The term *conflict resolution* is also used in a broad sense. *Resolution* is a process whereby the parties work out their disagreements in order to bring the conflict to a successful conclusion. The resolution process, too, can be either formal or informal. A formal resolution process may involve a meeting, or many meetings, between the parties. An informal process may be accomplished by brief communications between the parties, perhaps in the corridors or over the phone. Throughout the text, the terms *conflict resolution, bargaining, negotiation,* and *meetings* are all used interchangeably to refer to both the formal and the informal means people use to bring about successful conflict settlements.

Most conflicts are resolved at one of three levels: interest, rights, or power. At the *interest* level, the parties try to reach a settlement that satisfies the interests of the individuals involved. In other words, the parties ask what each individual needs in order to feel the disagreement is over. At this level, both parties should feel some degree of satisfaction from the settlement. At the *rights* level, each party is not interested in what the other needs; the issue is what each is entitled to under the law. Thus, lawyers and courts are apt to be involved at this level of conflict resolution. The *power* level of resolution involves parties that are trying to dominate each other. Here, the parties' relative strength is the key factor. Strikes, job actions, and harassment are all methods of conflict resolution at the level of power.

This book deals with conflict resolution at the interest level. The emphasis is on how two parties can successfully disengage from position statements and demands and, instead, focus on their real interests or needs. The book involves you in a process for resolving conflicts by expanding the interests of all parties involved. It is by clarifying what each party needs in order to be satisfied that the parties can come up with a settlement acceptable to all. The book offers a step-by-step description of various skills and tactics you can use during a conflict resolution process to achieve this end.

Many skills and tactics for conflict resolution are presented in this book. The description of each is usually followed by an example illustrating how to implement it. Activities are provided in each chapter to help you develop your own knowledge of how to put these skills into practice. In approaching this book, you should first read about a particular skill, then complete the activity associated with it, and then reflect on its applicability to your own experiences. Finally, try to implement the skill in a real conflict situation in which you are involved.

Experiment with implementing these tactics. Your first attempt may not be successful, but with practice and perhaps a re-reading of the relevant text you will gain a working knowledge of the skill. By integrating these skills with those you already possess and with your own style of administration, you can succeed in learning all the tactics presented in this book.

The first five chapters of this book are developed sequentially. The tactics described become more complex as you move through these first five chapters into the heart of the resolution process. The last two chapters relate to special issues of conflict and are designed to augment and enhance the bargaining skills you already possess. To help you, a case study called "Michael's Conflict" is described within each chapter to illustrate how the tactics presented apply to an actual conflict situation. A Conflict Resolution Guide at the end of each chapter lists the various tactics discussed in that chapter. The purpose of this guide is to help you apply the tactics to the specific conflict resolution situations in which you are involved. These guides can be easily reproduced for future use. For the reader interested in learning more about the particular topics discussed, a list of references is provided at the end of each chapter.

In Chapter One, you learn how to identify the sources and types of conflict that exist in schools. The theme of using your power to control conflict is discussed, especially as it relates to making the right decisions, overcoming your biases, and learning to persuade others. The developer model of persuasion is introduced as an effective framework within which to work out a successful settlement.

In Chapter Two you learn how to set the climate for talking about the conflict, how to prepare by establishing your purpose and role, and how to use the all-powerful BATNA (best alternative to a negotiated agreement).

Dealing with demands, anger, and threats is a necessary part of handling any conflict. Two conflict resolution tactics described in Chapter Three will give you some skills to deal with these issues.

In Chapter Four you will learn how to use pressure to move the other party to settle a conflict. You will learn ways to settle the conflict by exploring conflicting and common interests.

In Chapter Five the issue of how to get what you want out of a negotiation is discussed at length. Specifically, you will be shown how to use techniques to influence the other party, how to deal with concessions, and how to form a settlement that favors you without destroying the other party.

There is always the problem of how to deal with lies, deception, and game playing on the part of the other party. Although not all conflict resolution meetings involve such negative forces, the school administrator needs to be prepared to deal with them if they arise. In Chapter Six you will be shown how to use strategies to counter games and how to deal with those who are trying to manipulate the negotiations in a negative fashion.

In Chapter Seven you will gain an insight into your own style of administration and how this style affects the conflict resolution process. After completing the activities in this chapter, you will become aware of skills that will allow you to expand your administrative power and thereby become a more effective resolver of conflicts.

One final note is needed. In conflict resolution, there is never one correct method of dealing with the process. There is no one tactic that will work all the time in every conflict you attempt to resolve. I believe, however, that after reading this book you will never approach conflict in the same way. You will be more skillful and will have more confidence in your determination to handle any conflict that may come through your door.

CHAPTER ONE

Controlling Conflict with Power

As the old story goes, the worst time to be thinking about clearing the swamp is when you are up to your neck in alligators. For the school administrator, the worst time to be considering how to deal with conflict is when you are engulfed in one. Yet there is never a time when a school administrator can say that there are no controversial issues or potential conflict on the horizon. There is no right time to clear the swamp. Now is the time to plunge in and start to understand and implement conflict management strategies that work. That way, when the alligators come, you'll be ready.

This chapter views conflict in relation to power. Both are viewed as dynamic processes rather than static events. Both are ever changing and evolving as they interface with each other over the course of events. To be an effective resolver of conflicts, you must be able to use your power to have a positive influence on the outcome of a conflict. But first, let us look at the dynamics of conflict.

CONFLICT

Conflict is defined here as a disagreement resulting from incompatible demands between or among two or more parties. Conflict is not a state of being, but, rather, an active process, which over time takes on various dimensions and dynamics. The dynamics of conflict, however, are not random, erratic, or unpredictable series of events. If you have sufficient information about the conflict, you can see its order and patterns. From this viewpoint, conflict can then be seen as a process that can be intersected, influenced, and ultimately managed.

Why Is There Conflict in Education?

In meetings of school administrators one overhears any number of stories about conflict. Why is conflict so much a part of educational administration? Activity 1-1 lets you answer this question for yourself.

There are many answers to this question. One may be that the public views educators essentially as servants, whose job is to serve the children of the community. As service employees, then, our role is to be directed, to be open to criticism, and to be accountable. The problem arises because the role of teachers is not clearly defined. Are they skilled workers or are they professionals? How much autonomy and how much power do the community and the administration give to the teachers?

Another answer may be a widespread public skepticism about the efficiency of public education in general. Numerous reports from blue-ribbon panels, national commissions, and a host of popular books have contributed to a feeling that the professionals in charge of education are not minding the store and cannot even agree among themselves as to what should be done.

Still another answer may be that conflict is part of the very structure of schools, whether they are good schools or poor ones. Sara Lawrence Lightfoot, in *The Good High School* (New York: Basic Books, 1983, p. 24) talks about the ill-fated assumption that any school should be able to establish an atmosphere that satisfies all the individuals involved. She cites evidence that even the best schools show striking moments of vulnerability, inconsistency, and awkwardness.

Conflict may exist in schools because they are organizations with inherently mixed motives. Different teachers in the same building may view testing, to take one example, in entirely different ways. For some it may be a way of determining who has been attentive, a way of sorting students, or even a mode of punishment.

ACTIVITY 1-1

WHY IS CONFLICT SO PREVALENT IN EDUCATION TODAY?

Take a minute to write down your own thoughts about this question. You might ask a colleague the question, too. At the next educational conference you attend, listen to what the keynote speaker says about the problems of education. Review the titles of articles in the various educational professional journals. What do they tell you about common problems in education? Compare all these answers to the one you wrote down. How do you agree with each of them and how do you disagree?

_____

_____

_____

_____

_____

_____

For others it may be a way of getting feedback about students varying abilities to grasp the way the course is taught.

Finally, questions about the goals or interests of a school are a common source of conflict. How these and other questions about the school as an organization are answered determines, in part, the nature of the conflicts that will arise.

In any conflict there are antecedent conditions that may be at the root of the initial dispute. These conditions may not cause the full-blown conflict, but they are strong enough to start the process on its way. A few of them are:

- Ambiguous roles
- Conflicting interests
- Communication barriers (distance, time, prejudices)
- Dependence of one party
- Differentiation of organization
- Need for consensus

- Behavior regulations or rules
- Unresolved prior conflicts

   The lack of certain conditions can also be a cause of conflict. A few examples are listed here.

- Lack of trust
- Lack of integrity
- Lack of benefits
- Lack of information
- Lack of clarity

These conditions will be discussed at length in Chapter Two. You can then determine which of these conditions existed in any previous conflict (Activity 1-2).

IDENTIFYING TYPES OF CONFLICT

There are three main types of conflict a school administrator may encounter. These have been described analytically by Clyde H. Coombs in "The Structure of Conflict," *American Psychologist*, Vol. 42, April 1987, pp. 355–363. A summary of each type of conflict follows.

Type I: Parties Have Incompatible Goals

This kind of conflict can involve a single person struggling to make a decision between two different goals or outcomes—for example, having to decide which birthday party to attend when two parties fall on the same night. Or the conflict may involve two or more parties who each must choose an outcome, but whose goals are incompatible. For example, suppose you and your spouse decide to buy a new dishwasher. You want the cheaper, more energy-efficient model, but your spouse prefers the quieter, more expensive model. In either type of situation, you must choose between two or more possible goals.

   A relevant example of this type of conflict is seen in the decision one school administrator must make in scheduling students. Students in this school have a wide range of ability levels. Most of the students at lower ability levels are also minority students. The administrator must decide whether to group the students according to ability levels or according to a heterogeneous mix of students

---

ACTIVITY 1-2

Consider a recent conflict in your school. In attempting to identify the cause of this conflict, consider the series of questions given here. Record your response to each question by circling the appropriate answer to the right.

1. Did the participants act according to the role expected? (For example, was the administrator performing supervisory activities, the teacher involved in teaching, the parent acting as an effective parent, and so on?)

   YES   NO

2. Did the participants have a clear sense of the issues involved in the conflict?

   YES   NO

3. Did the participants share with each other their real interest in the issues?

   YES   NO

4. Did these interests conflict in some manner?

   YES   NO

5. Were the participants able to talk to each other about their differing interests?

   YES   NO

6. Was one of the participants dependent on the other in any way?

   YES   NO

7. Did the participants need to come to a consensus in their decision making?

   YES   NO

8. Were the school's rules or policies misunderstood, not adhered to, or not known to one of the participants?

   YES   NO

9. Was there a history of conflict between the participants prior to the recent conflict?

   YES   NO

10. Was there an unresolved conflict prior to the present one?

    YES   NO

11. Was sufficient time allowed for this conflict to be resolved?

YES   NO

How many times did you circle NO? _____

If you circled more than three NOs, you can be sure there were very strong antecedent conditions at the root of this present conflict. That means there were issues present prior to the conflict that exerted a significant force to help provoke the conflict.

In thinking ahead, look at each of the criteria listed here and consider which items could possibly be the cause of any number of future conflicts. These factors may represent the beginnings of a conflict. Moving quickly and applying the tactics described in this book may help you manage that possible conflict.

of different races. These grouping procedures are incompatible with each other. The administrator who groups according to ability has, in effect, segregated the school. Yet the one who groups heterogeneously may be depriving the brighter students of a challenging classroom atmosphere. This is a decision involving *values*.

Type I conflict between parties can be seen in the decision to deny a teacher tenure. If a teacher wants tenure at the school, but the superintendent wants to deny tenure, their goals obviously are mutually incompatible. This is a decision involving *measurement*.

Many Type I conflicts involve decisions based either on ethics or on issues of measurement. Because the goals or outcomes are incompatible, the usual method of resolving conflicts is to have an outside judge or higher level administrator make the decision. No matter what this person decides, one party will be seen as the winner and the other as the loser.

Type II: Parties Want Different Things but Must Settle on One Solution

In Type II conflicts the parties are required to find a mutually acceptable solution that satisfies the needs of all concerned. Unlike Type I conflicts, these do not involve incompatible goals. The solution to Type II conflicts may lie with finding an alternative outcome.

An example of a Type II conflict is seen in a conflict that the school principal must mediate. A teacher wants to give a failing grade to a student, but the student's parents are demanding that the grade be an A because, they say, the teacher is prejudiced. The two parties to this conflict want different things, but both parties must agree on one solution. At first glance it may seem that the two stated goals are incompatible, but they are not. In fact, a solution can be found that will satisfy both parties.

To solve Type II conflicts, there must be a sense of community, a need to preserve the bond between the parties, an ability to persuade the parties, and some mutual interest in resolving the conflict. This type of conflict can involve a win or gain for both parties. Therefore, most conflicts should be resolved at the Type II level.

Type III: Parties Want the Same Thing, but Only One Can Have It

In this type of conflict, both parties want the same thing, but only one can have it. Type III conflicts are the most dangerous type. Left alone, these conflicts get out of control, with an escalation of violent actions and reactions.

An example found in schools occurs when central office personnel would like to take over a school building shed to store lawnmowers, but the school building personnel want to use the same shed for the student council office. The building-level people claim that because the shed is on the school building grounds, its use should be up to the school, not the district. The central office claims that because the school's lawn is cut by the lawnmowers, if the school personnel want the lawn cut, they had better let the mowers be stored in the shed. This conflict is not resolved quickly. Instead, it escalates. The student council officers "occupy" the shed and expose the conflict in the student newspaper. In response, the central office building and grounds office refuses to cut the school's lawn.

Type III conflicts lead to confrontation involving self-interests and the use of brute power to gain the desired solution. What is needed instead is a negotiation involving mutual interests and persuasion. To solve Type III conflicts, it is necessary to transform them into Type II conflicts. A referee may be needed to do this. Unless the parties involved begin to find mutual interests in resolving this conflict, however, it will only get worse.

In Activity 1-3, you have a chance to identify actual conflicts of all three types that you have confronted in the past.

ACTIVITY 1-3

Each of the three conflict types are listed here. Identify one conflict of each type that you have had to manage in the past. Write the sequence of events here and explain why you think the conflict belonged to that specific type.

Type I: _____

_____

_____

Type II: _____

_____

_____

Type III: _____

_____

_____

    Of the three different conflicts listed, which was the easiest and which was the hardest to resolve? Which type of conflict led to escalation? Finally, which conflict could have been transformed into a different type?

How Conflict Erupts in Schools

Hindsight can be a powerful teacher. Often, we wish we had known then what we know now. Perhaps the conflict would not have consumed so much time and energy, or involved so much stress, if we could have predicted its onslaught early on. This section describes one method of viewing the stages of a conflict. For further reading in this area, see *When It Hits the Fan: Managing the Nine Crises of Business,* by Gerald C. Meyers (New York: NAL Penguin, 1986). In one sense these stages are predictable, linear, and highly destructive.

Phase I: The Smoke

This is the initial stage of the conflict, where the pattern of events starts to take shape, the specific actors start to assume roles, and interests become hardened. Usually the conflict begins with something that is not working as it should. There is a period of poor or even nonexistent performance. Perhaps a school policy is not being enforced consistently, or a staff member has decided to let things slip in the classroom. When alerted to this potential problem, the administrator has two choices: to acknowledge the inconsistency and attempt to deal with it or to deny the evidence that points to a problem and simply allow the problem to fester and perhaps even grow. In the former case the administrator will attempt to resolve the conflict early on. In the latter case the problem will continue to develop until it erupts in the form of angry outbursts or in expressions of fear among the staff.

Resolving a conflict during its initial stage is much easier than resolving it later on, when the firestorm is raging. One way to detect smoke is to use the famous management skill advocated in the book *In Search of Excellence* by Thomas J. Peters and Robert H. Waterman (New York: Harper & Row, 1982, p. 122). They call this skill MBWA—"managing by walking about." A school administrator who schedules time to be in the hallways, time to talk with teachers in the staff rooms and classrooms, and time to meet with parents is in a position to detect smoke as soon as it arises. This administrator will rarely be surprised by a full-fledged storm of conflict raging outside the office door, because he or she has a full understanding of the pressures, the gossip, and the mood of the schools.

Phase II: The Fire

Trouble arises when there is a breakdown in the system that has been established to protect school personnel from such conflict. The immediate negative response to trouble is usually panic. School administrators are apt to circle the wagons and try to ride out the storm. They schedule endless conferences to find out what happened. Some may be angry because they feel they were not informed that smoke was visible earlier on. Others fear that the conflict will engulf them. In fact, they are right. Unless something proactive is done to deal with the conflict, the fire will eventually consume them, and the system, or at least part of the system, will collapse.

The most positive immediate response is one of clear and concise action. The school administrator should gather information and try to assess the causes of the conflict and the issues involved in it. They should not try to deny that a conflict exists, nor should they let themselves become overwrought with anxiety about it. School administrators who have a positive outlook toward conflict know, because of their track record, that they will be able to resolve the conflict before it is too destructive. They are able to issue clear directions, which start the process of resolution.

Phase III: The Ashes

Once the fury of the conflict has subsided, a period of reassessment follows. Considerable time may elapse before the conflict has run its course. When this period ends, the administrator who has reacted negatively is likely to be in a state of shock, facing a period of uncertainty and probably of radical change. The superintendent may be out of a job, or the building principal may find long-range performance objectives awaiting his implementation.

For the school administrator who reacted in a positive manner, however, there will now be a period of recovery and probably of reform. The system need not be restructured because the system was never destroyed. People did not lose their jobs as a result of the problem. Nevertheless, new things definitely must be accomplished. The school system must be made more responsive to people's concerns. It must develop a climate in which conflict is used to develop positive changes in the system.

How Not to Handle Conflict: An Example

The conflict arose suddenly. Yet anyone who taught in the high school could have predicted the turmoil that befell this large urban school district. For years this high school had reported to the state education department quite praiseworthy achievement test scores. On statewide exams in both math and reading, the number of students who were passing the minimum competency level had been increasing until, for the past few years, the rate was 95 percent of the senior class. This high rate was in itself not extraordinary. Most schools in this state had rates as high or higher. Yet the problem with this particular high school was that the staff did not believe that the students performed that well in the daily classes. They saw a wide discrepancy between the students' reported accomplishments and what they were actually doing in their classes.

The English teachers asked the school principal to attend a meeting to question the high test results. The principal had delegated the scoring of the tests to one of the assistant principals, a long-time staff member who was older than the principal. When asked about the English teachers' comments, the assistant principal dismissed the teachers as meddlesome. He then claimed that he had copies of all the exams available for anyone to view. No one took him up on this offer, however, and the principal dropped the issue.

The Smoke

In this case, the principal received complaints from members of his staff. Yet he chose to ignore the existence of this "smoke." He denied that there was a problem simply because his assistant told him so. In fact, the assistant told the principal exactly what he wanted to hear—and he did.

The Fire

The "fire" stage of this conflict began when the state education department asked to review the completed exams as part of a routine spot-check program. When the assistant principal could not find all the copies of the exams for each of several years, he blamed his secretary for the messiness of the storage system. Thus, the principal again denied the smoke, although he did become upset with his assistant because he now had to write a letter explaining the situation to the education department. The fire raged further when the department sent an investigator to audit the exam results. The audit could not take place, however, because the records were missing. But some of the teachers began telling the investigator of their own doubts about the high test results.

When the principal informed the superintend of schools of the situation, the superintendent reacted first with anger at the principal and then with fear because of the growing publicity. The superintendent called a meeting of his immediate assistants. Taking a circle-the-wagons approach, he delegated responsibility for helping with the investigation to one of these assistants and then dismissed the whole affair as a problem of housekeeping. His aim was to put as much distance between himself and the mess as possible.

The third stage of the raging firestorm was the formal letter to the superintendent from the state director of education citing the school district as being in noncompliance with education department regulations. The district's state aid for education was held up pending a final report on the testing policies of the district.

Upon receiving this letter, the superintendent panicked. He claimed total ignorance of the problem and tried to lay the blame for the situation on the building-level principal and the assistant principal. But the board of education would not hear it.

The Ashes

The "ashes" stage of this conflict was a time of shock as the details of the testing fraud were reported in the local newspapers. For a while there was some uncertainty as to how far the damage would go. No one in the district thought about merely reforming the testing procedures. Everyone wanted to tear down the façade of the system that had been allowed to exist. Radical change was demanded, and radical change occurred.

In the aftermath of this conflict, the superintendent lost his job, the assistant principal was forced to retire, the principal was demoted to a go-fer job in the central office, two school board members lost in their reelection bids, and the education department monitored the district's test operations for the next five years.

Hindsight

Had the principal been more active in his building, he would have heard about the teachers' complaints long before the English teachers held a formal meeting on the subject. In any case, once a formal meeting was called, that should have prompted the principal to investigate immediately. Although the smoke was everywhere, the superintendent still probably could have saved himself if he had taken more deliberate action. He should have seen the smoke and carried out his own investigation promptly. He should have issued directions and taken a proactive role in the conflict. The school district would have faced some difficulties because of the fraud, but the damage might have been controlled, and the district administrators, except for the assistant principal, might have recovered and remained to reform the system.

POWER

Now that we have gained a better understanding of the nature of conflict, let's look at what we mean by power. *Power* is defined as the functional ability to make others commit themselves to a course of action. Power, like conflict, is a process, not a state of being. You do not possess power; rather, you function with power. It is the way you influence events that defines whether you are using power. The mere fact that superintendents are appointed to office does not mean that they have power to influence events. A superintendent's constituents will view the effectiveness of the position as defined by the actions taken over time to influence events.

Suppose that as a building principal you discover that one of the teachers is failing 25 percent of her class. Parents and students are complaining. The teacher also is complaining to you about these complaints and about her rights as a teacher. Clearly, here is a conflict that needs to be managed.

The principal must decide at what point she wants to enter the conflict. She may act early in the conflict, at the complaint stage, or later, at the formal grievance stage, or anywhere in the course of the unfolding conflict. The decisions the principal makes and the way she persuades the parties involved to solve the dispute will determine the efficiency with which she uses her power.

You need to understand the source of your power because it is in the use of your power that you are able to intersect with and influence conflict. Activity 1-4 includes a list of some common sources of power. Take a minute or two to complete this list.

The two most important sources of your power are the last two on the checklist—the ability to make the right decisions and the ability to persuade others. Because these two sources are so crucial, the remainder of this chapter will give you an in-depth understanding of how to use them more effectively.

How to Make the Right Decisions

Most people think that the process of making decisions involves a series of steps, following one another in a logical sequence, each leading to a successful conclusion on the basis of which an intelligent decision can be made. These steps are typically something like this:

- Assessing the challenge
- Brainstorming possible solutions
- Analyzing each solution
- Choosing the best solution
- Implementing the solution
- Publicly disclosing the decision

ACTIVITY 1-4

Check those sources of power that pertain to your position and explain why you think you have power from each of these sources. Be specific. Describe what you do and what happens as a result of this action.

1. Power from providing resources   _____

2. Power from having political connections   _____

3. Power from coping with uncertainty   _____

4. Power from being irreplaceable   _____

5. Power from gaining consensus   _____

6. Power from getting things done   _____

7. Power from affecting decisions   _____

8. Power from persuading others   _____

    Total number of checks   _____

    If you have checked at least two of these sources, you may consider yourself equipped with sufficient power to control conflict. If you have checked more than two, you have an extra advantage and a positive likelihood for success in controlling conflict.

Although this process may be the ideal, most school administrators, like most successful business managers, rarely invoke the entire process in reaching a decision. School administrators make decisions on the basis of the relationship of various factors—time, money, resources, energy, and the importance of the decision at the moment. If an angry parent is on the phone at 3:30 P.M. on a Friday, the administrator is more likely to make a decision based on fatigue and lack of time than one based on a careful assessment of all the available information about the problem. How administrators make decisions—and successful ones at that—without using the full decision-making process is the secret of their success. They do it by thinking on their feet.

In careful studies of how managers reach decisions (Daniel J. Isenberg, "Thinking and Managing: A Verbal Protocol Analysis of Managerial Problem Solving," *Academy of Management Journal*,

Vol. 29, 1986, pp. 775–788), it has been found that most managers start making decisions about problems relatively early in the conflict. They do not spend a lot of time gathering all the available information about the problem before moving into action. They know how to reason from analogy—that is, from past experiences. Thus, they compare the basic facts of the current problem with problems they have faced in the past. They use their intuition to draw inferences, build some contingencies, and act. Later, on the basis of feedback they receive from their initial decision, they may need to adjust the decision and make some minor additions. The decision is adjusted as it is implemented, and the end product is a carefully implemented decision, which resolves the problem successfully. Some people call this process *thinking/acting.* Others call it "thinking on your feet." It is a process all administrators use every day, but they are often unaware that they are using a fairly sophisticated information-processing system.

All successful decisions dealing with conflict have some common factors. These factors can be summarized in the following statement.

The right policy with observable action goals

As you consider your decision, compare it to the factors in this statement. How does it measure against this standard? Look at each factor in turn.

Right

Does your decision address what common sense dictates as the proper, decent, and ethical thing to do? To use an old adage, would your mother approve of your decision?

Policy

Does your decision deal with a matter of principle, or does it deal with a unique event? Are you establishing a policy with your decision? If so, be sure it can be used by others as a standard by which to judge other cases. If your decision deals with a single issue, then it need not be so general in scope. The wise administrator knows how to delegate decisions about unique events to other staff members. Your own energy and time should be devoted to decisions that make policy.

Observable

To get feedback on your decision, you need to see its effects. If you are the type of administrator described here, who thinks and acts at the same time, then you especially need accurate feedback about your decision to enable you to make mid-course corrections.

Action

The hardest part of any decision is implementation. Every decision needs an action plan that is timely and feasible. This aspect of decision making takes the most time and requires most patience on your part.

Goals

Will your decision have an outcome? Is something going to happen that will change things? You should be able to say that, as a result of your decision, some objective will be met at some time in the future.

Think about the last important decision you had to make. What was the issue involved? Who represented the various sides of the problem? What were the opposing arguments? What was your final word on the subject? Now take that decision and compare it to the statements in Activity 1-5.

Determining Your Bias

Because administrators make so many decisions on their feet, they often take short cuts that expedite their information processing. Early on, they make assumptions about the presenting problem and arrive at generalizations based on past experiences. Although these decisions are likely to be accurate, there are also some dangers involved. These dangers arise from the systematic biases that the administrator brings to the situation. A *bias* is a perception about a problem that is not related to the facts of the particular case. Making a decision on the basis of a bias can lead you down the wrong road, perhaps even a destructive one, in trying to solve a problem. A few of these biases are discussed next.

ACTIVITY 1-5

In this activity, compare your most recent tough decision to the standard. By *tough* we mean a decision that you took some time to make because of the many competing issues involved.

How was it *right*? _____

_____

_____

_____

On what *policy* was it based? _____

_____

_____

_____

How was it *observable*? _____

_____

_____

_____

What *action* was taken? _____

_____

_____

_____

What were the *goals*? _____

_____

_____

_____

After completing this section, review your answers and determine how you could have made your decision more successful using these criteria.

Bias Based on Overconfidence

People generally are overconfident about their chances of success when they are trying to resolve a problem in their favor. Most people think they can be 100 percent correct in making a decision. Statistically, however, your odds of getting the solution you want are never 100 percent. Regardless of the exact odds, overconfidence can be a problem if it biases your decision making.

You have all heard those teachers in the staff room who loudly proclaim that they will be able to persuade the principal to see things their way. They exhibit tremendous overconfidence in approaching a problem. This overconfidence is a bias that clouds their ability to resolve the problem because it decreases their willingness to make compromises necessary to reach a settlement. When their proposed solutions meet resistance, such people often become angry and withdraw from the negotiations.

In making decisions about a problem, it is always wise to remember that you may have to make concessions or compromises along the way in order to achieve your goals.

Bias Based on Negative Perception

People who make decisions on the basis of what they expect to lose in a situation are likely to make few concessions and are more apt to have their problem-solving efforts reach an impasse. By contrast, those who approach a decision with a positive mind set, ex-

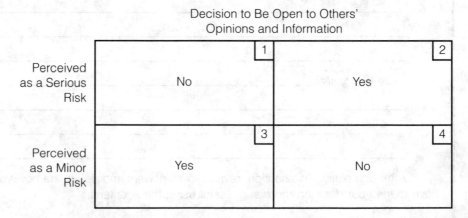

Figure 1-1. Conflict Decision-Making Matrix

pecting to *gain* something from the situation, are likely to make concessions and, in the process, to achieve their goals.

Take the example of the teachers' union negotiator who is trying to keep certain clauses in the contract from being removed. Because he does not want to give up any negotiated gains, he will make few concessions during negotiations and will resist any attempts to alter the written contract. He will be willing to reach an impasse in an effort to preserve what he has. On the other hand, consider the union negotiator who is looking for gains for his teachers. He is willing to give up any particular clause in the contract if he can turn that concession into a more significant gain elsewhere in the contract. He perceives the negotiation as a process of making decisions about teachers' *interests,* rather than about teachers' possessions as stipulated in the contract.

Bias Based on Perception of Risk

The administrator's perception of risk during a conflict is a key factor in determining how many other individual opinions should be sought. This opinion search opens the administrator to other ideas about the problem and its possible solutions. Figure 1-1 illustrates this matrix of decision making.

On the left-hand side of the figure is the administrator's perception of the risk involved in the conflict. Is this conflict a minor or a major problem to be solved? On the top of the matrix is the administrator's relative openness to others' opinions and ideas about the problem. Within each of the quadrants is a decision the administrator must make with regard to seeking the opinions of others.

In quadrant 1 the administrator perceives a serious risk in the conflict and is not open to others' opinions. This situation occurs when there is a crisis that calls for immediate attention and a quick decision. It also opens the way for the most dangerous type of decision making. Without feedback from others the administrator is taking a chance, assuming that his or her decision will be accurate and will solve the problem successfully.

In quadrant 2 the administrator perceives the conflict as risky but does decide to seek others' opinions before resolving the situation. Here, the administrator sees the conflict resolution process in a positive light, as a challenge.

In quadrant 3 the administrator perceives the conflict as a minor risk, yet nevertheless decides to seek the opinions of others.

Playing it safe in this way significantly reduces the chances of failure.

In quadrant 4 the administrator perceives the conflict as minor and decides not to seek others' opinions. The problem here is that the perception that the risk is minor may be wrong. Without outside feedback, the administrator may make a decision that will later backfire.

Bias Based on Personality

A decision can be flawed if it is based on the individuals involved rather than on the merits of the case. This type of bias is tricky because we do have to deal with the person behind the problem as well as with the problem itself. Trying to deal specifically with the person, however, can make us lose sight of the problem and of the best solution. Sooner or later everyone has the experience of sitting across from someone during a conflict resolution meeting and thinking that the person opposite is totally out of touch with reality. Perhaps the person says things that seem absurd or has irritating personal mannerisms. There is a tendency to dismiss what such a person has to say because it is so easy to dismiss the person. A few simple guidelines can help keep your focus on the problem, not the person.

First, remember as you deal with people that they have personal needs. These needs should be addressed along with any substantive issues involved. How a solution fulfills someone's personal needs may be just as important as the issue itself. In decision making, ask yourself whether, when the negotiation is over, the person will feel that his or her interests have been addressed. It is appropriate to have the person in question determine this simply by asking: "Does this solution meet your needs?"

Emotions are a part of all negotiations. People get angry, get depressed, feel elated. All the normal emotions can and should be present at a meeting. Expect them to surface. When they do present themselves, you have a choice in how you decide to deal with them. You can ignore them, acknowledge them, or try to change them. If you choose to ignore them, you do not have to deal with the feelings or embarrass the other person, who in most cases just wants to ventilate the feelings and does not want to deal with them any more than you do. If the emotion expressed is particularly strong, it is wise to acknowledge it by saying simply, "I understand you are angry (or sad, or happy) about this." If you try to deal with the emotion expressed, you may divert the discussion from its original purpose. Sometimes, however, it is necessary to discuss the whys and hows of a person's feelings before any substantive issue can be raised. In some cases, then, dealing with a person's feelings about an issue is as important as dealing with the issue.

Your own feelings are important in any decision-making process as well. You should communicate these feelings to the other person. Use "I" statements to let the other person know where you stand on an issue—for example, "I feel good about this decision" or "This decision makes me feel lousy." Also, by communicating where you stand, you are modelling for the other person a way of placing your feelings out in the open. In this process, the issue may become clearer and the solution easier to address to meet everyone's needs.

How to Persuade Others

In addition to the power of making decisions, the administrator also has the power to persuade. This is a very real source of functional power. In many cases of conflict management, the administrator needs to be able to change people's minds about an issue in order to reach a settlement. The effective administrator is a persuader who can get people to change.

There are five different models of persuasion, as shown in Activity 1-6. No one uses one model exclusively, but there is a tendency to favor one model over another depending on the particular situation. In most cases, an administrator will attempt to change someone using one model but, upon meeting any substantial resistance, will employ pieces of other models to support the case for change. Deciding which model to use is entirely up to the administrator and for that reason reflects the administrator's power base. For more information, see J. R. P. French and B. Raven, "The Bases of Social Power," *Studies in Social Power,* edited by D. Cartwright (Ann Arbor: Institute for Social Research, University of Michigan, 1959).

Model 1: Sanction Model

This model uses rewards and punishments to change people. It makes compliance a factor in eliciting a punishment or a reward. For example, an assistant principal might say to one of the social studies teachers on duty in the cafeteria:

___ **ACTIVITY 1-6** ___

Here is a short questionnaire that will give you examples of a number of situations involving persuasion. After each item there is a letter in parentheses. Of the two situations presented together, choose the one that most closely resembles your own manner of persuasion. Assume that all the information presented is true.

You are trying to persuade a teacher to take Room 301, the classroom most in need of remodeling of any in the building, for the next school year:

1. You point out to the teacher that if she takes Room 301, she will get the morning sunshine in her windows and her plants will thrive.   (E)

or

2. You offer the teacher Room 301 but promise her that she will have no cafeteria duty if she takes the room.   (B)

Letter chosen _____

You are trying to settle a dispute about a grade on the final report card:

3. You direct the teacher to change the grade to reflect the true average that appears in the teacher's roll book.   (D)

or

4. You explain to the teacher that according to your calculations, the grades in the roll book do not reflect the falling grade he gave the student. You point out the discrepancy and ask the teacher to explain the difference.   (DV)

Letter chosen _____

As superintendent, you are trying to get an elementary school principal to attend more PTA meetings:

5. You tell the principal that even though she has tenure and you cannot fire her, you do expect her to attend monthly PTA meetings, and that failure to do so will result in a letter in her file.   (S)

or

6. You make a compromise with the principal. She can have fewer parent coffee open houses at the school during the day if she will attend the monthly evening PTA meetings.   (B)

Letter chosen _____

Place the three letters chosen for each of the three situations on the lines below.

——————— ——————— ———————

These letters represent different forms of persuasion that are available to a school administrator. They stand for:

E: Expert advice model

B: Bargaining model

D: Directive model

DV: Developer model

S: Sanction model

There is no right or wrong model of persuasion. In each of these situations, the model you chose represented a forced choice. In reality you might have chosen some other form of persuasion. The point of this activity is to illustrate the fact that persuasion depends on the situation. How you decide to persuade someone to change depends on a host of factors. These factors are discussed following a description of the different models of persuasion.

If you do not arrive on time, I will have to write you up on this unprofessional behavior.

As a reward sanction, the statement might be:

If you can come on time, I'll make sure you do not get this duty again next year.

The advantage of the sanction model is that it generally achieves instant results. Change takes place with little expenditure of time and personal involvement. One disadvantage is that the other person sees the change as being imposed and manipulative. The locus of control is seen as being outside the person. Therefore, the change will not be permanent, and the performance demanded will most likely not be excellent. A second, related disadvantage is that the administrator will need to monitor the change to make sure it sticks. A third disadvantage is that the person in question will feel some strain in relations with the administrator, especially if there is punishment involved. You may win the behavior change but lose the heart of the person.

Despite its disadvantages, this model of persuasion is often used in schools to manage conflict. Although some may question its professionalism, it is needed at times and is, indeed, an essential model of persuasion.

Model 2: Directive Model

With this model the school administrator actually directs or orders the other person to change. This may involve such tactics as being assertive or even invoking board of education policies or state education law. The imposition of budget constraints is another example of using a legitimate outside source to compel change.

Using assertive tactics, the department chair may say to the teacher:

Now, I have listened to all your arguments about why you want this textbook series. However, I have decided for the good of all to order the other series. There will be no more discussion of this matter. Thank you for your input.

Using the constraints of the law, a superintendent may say to a board member:

There is absolutely no way we can do that without being sued. The law is clear about these matters. I request that we try an alternative approach.

Other forms of direction using this model employ phrases such as "I would like you to . . . ," "Could you please . . . ," or "I request that you . . ."

The advantage of this model is that it delivers a firm, clear request for change. There is no question about which way the decision will go. The use of an assertive command will make the other people involved feel that the locus of control is outside themselves. They may feel compelled to change but will not believe in the merits of the change. The legal or budgetary constraints approach is more effective because it places the locus of control outside *both* parties involved in the dispute. It is hard to continue the argument if there is an outside source exerting power.

One disadvantage of this form of persuasion is that it necessitates some monitoring for compliance. A second disadvantage is that the administrator may have to use threats or bluffs to impose the desired directive.

Model 3: Bargaining Model

Compromise is the focus of the bargaining model of persuasion, in which the two parties involved in the dispute decide to break even and split the difference between them. In some cases this may mean a trade-off, or perhaps a postponement or a curtailing of any gains sought.

A dialogue between a principal and an assistant superintendent utilizing trade-offs in the bargaining model might include a statement like this:

> *Listen, I am willing to reschedule my achievement tests to schedule this district-wide science fair, but I will require a promise from you that the fair will not be held in my building.*

A statement from another dialogue between two principals illustrates a compromise in which each receives less than originally asked for.

> *I will compromise with you on this. I would like school next year to start at 9:00 A.M., but you wish it to start at 8:30 A.M. Suppose we agree on 8:45 A.M.*

The advantage of this model is that no one really loses. It is a win–win approach because everyone is involved in some way in the decision-making process. Because the locus of control is within each of the participants, the change will be more permanent. Little monitoring of the change will be required because there was total involvement of all parties in the decision.

The disadvantage, of course, is that often all parties walk away with less than they asked for. Compromise means giving in order to get. It is the giving that constitutes a loss. After the settlement, then, there may be some resentment. The parties may return to the bargaining table at some future date to try to regain whatever they gave up earlier.

Model 4: The Expert Advice Model

Some administrators are more knowledgeable about some matters than others are. Experience is often the source of such knowledge.

At administrative meetings participants often rely on the advice of the more senior members. Some administrators are viewed as particularly good writers or speakers, and they will be called on to use their talents at different times. These are all examples of using expert advice in order to produce change. Outside consultants are viewed as experts and are often called in to help resolve disputes. Mediators are another type of expert, who can provide advice that helps the parties reach a settlement.

In the following example, the principal uses the expert advice model to try to get a student's parents to give up a request to have their son changed from one teacher to another.

> *I understand your desire that your daughter be with the same teacher that her friends have. However, I can assure you that her present English teacher is a master, absolutely a master, at teaching students the process of creative writing. In all my years of experience I have not seen such a job so well done.*

The advantage of the expert advice model is that the locus of control is seen to reside with someone who has more information, experience, or know-how. The parties involved can readily give up their claim to a demand if the expert assures them that there are other, better ways to do things. The change then becomes an internalized process based on a cognitive decision.

The chief disadvantage of this model is that it relies on all parties placing their trust in the expert. They need to believe the source of advice. If one of the parties in the dispute is trying to act as an expert, the other party may have a problem in giving that trust. Nevertheless, the expert advice model is a common form of persuasion used in schools.

Model 5: The Developer Model

The last model of persuasion in our series is the most sophisticated. It is fast becoming popular in educational circles because of the long-lasting positive change that it brings about. This model involves the dissemination of information to support a position, the exploration of the various interests and values in a dispute, and the gradual building of a consensus of opinion about one settlement option. The administrator who uses this model acts as a catalyst or influencer. The administrator must encourage others to express opinions and values, must be willing to experiment and seek creative ways to solve problems on the basis of facts and reason rather than a preconceived position, and must demonstrate openness toward other views and try to gain consensus about a change. Using this model, the administrator will persuade others by reaching decisions through a blending of ideas rather than by directive.

This model is illustrated in the following example, where the principal is addressing a faculty about the need to raise student expectations.

As you can see from the handout I gave you, our test results show some good news and some bad news. We need to improve student writing abilities in this building. That is evident. I am open to any ideas that can lead to this result. In the next few weeks I will be meeting with you in small groups to discuss your ideas. I am open to any idea, so please give it some thought.

The advantage of this type of persuasion is that it internalizes the change process and, as a result, allows all parties to feel they have a part in it. As a result, the change tends to be longer lasting. Also, the quality of change tends to be high because many ideas have been brought to the process and only the best have been chosen. There is little need to monitor the change because everyone has agreed to it from the outset.

The disadvantage is that this process takes time. It involves building influence among staff members, using that influence over time, and sustaining it in the daily decisions an administrator makes. Not every instance of persuasion needs to follow this model. No school building or district could be run entirely using this model. But major policy decisions, for example, are important enough for this model to be implemented.

Comparison of Persuasion Models

Figure 1-2 compares the five models of persuasion in terms of three factors: personal satisfaction, the feeling of being in control of the change, and the absence of the need to monitor the change (nonmonitoring). Level 5 indicates a high presence of each of these factors. Level 1 indicates a low presence of each factor. For instance, at level 1 there would be a low level of personal satisfaction, a low level of feeling in control, and a high level of monitoring of the

High Level of			Low Level of	
Satisfaction			Satisfaction	
Control			Control	
Nonmonitoring			Nonmonitoring	
5	4	3	2	1
Developer	Expert	Bargaining	Directive	Sanction

FIGURE 1-2. Comparison of Persuasion Models

change being implemented (in other words, a low level of non-monitoring). It is evident that the developer model rates the highest in terms of satisfaction, control, and nonmonitoring.

Activity 1-7 gives you an opportunity to reflect on some recent instances of persuasion in your own experience. Which model of persuasion did you use? Why did you choose this model?

Factors Influencing Choice of Persuasion Model

What are the factors that affect which persuasion model you use? Here are some:

Time

Time is probably the most influential factor. It takes time to persuade others to adopt a change. You may not have enough time to achieve your goals in the "best" way. In emergencies, you need to be able to issue an order and expect that it will be followed. Expediency is sometimes more important than diplomacy. In less pressing cases, however, you need to reflect on which form of persuasion to use. You need to take the time to choose a persuasion procedure that meets the needs of everyone involved.

Boss–Subordinate Roles

You would be unlikely to use a directive style of persuasion with your boss, nor would you attempt to threaten him or her to elicit support for change. Here, common sense dictates that you try the developer model or perhaps the expert advice model. Using the expert advice model tends to make the boss dependent on you. If you

ACTIVITY 1-7

This activity lists the five persuasion models discussed in this chapter. Think about the past week and the decisions you made that involved persuading others to do certain things. These decisions may involve a secretary, a teacher, a department chair, a fellow administrator, or even your boss. In each case, decide which model of persuasion you used to influence this party to do something. Then determine for yourself why you chose a particular persuasion model. Refer to the factors discussed in the text to help you as you complete the following worksheet.

Sanction model _____

_____

_____

_____

Reason for decision _____

_____

Directive model _____

_____

_____

_____

Reason for decision _____

_____

Bargaining model _____

_____

_____

_____

Reason for decision _____

_____

Expert advice model _____

_____

_____

_____

Reason for decision _____

_____

Developer model _____

_____

_____

Reason for decision _____

_____

---

are the boss, you may be more apt to use the sanction or directive model to get results. You are less likely to view your subordinates as people you need to persuade to do something. Instead, you simply expect that they will do it.

Objectives Involved

At times you may be most interested in achieving a certain goal or objective. How it gets done, how long it takes, and who is involved are all less important than accomplishing the goal. If this is the case, the developer model may be the best one to use. The more involved in the change staff members feel, the more likely they are to feel the change as coming from within themselves, and the more durable the change will be. Sanction models, by contrast, usually produce change only while thc sanction is in effect.

Costs

There are costs involved in implementing any of the persuasion models. Here, *cost* is used to mean actual dollar amounts. In general, the more time is spent in persuading, the more costly the process becomes. The developer model, because it relies on generating information and forming a consensus, is particularly costly at first. However, sanction models are costly also because of the monitoring that needs to accompany the change over a long period. In the bargaining model, which involves compromise and giving in order to get, whatever is given up costs something.

Peer Groups

With parents the administrator may attempt to use the developer model in the hope that such a rational process will be most likely to produce change. Many school administrators approach parents as peers in their children's education. Parents respect this attitude, which makes them feel that they have an important part to play, as in fact they do. At times, however, the sanction model may need to be applied in dealing with a parent. Cases of child abuse, truancy, or drug dependency may require that the administrator invoke the law and threaten parents.

In dealings with fellow administrators, the developer model and the bargaining model are the most prevalent. With the developer model, the administrators attempt to persuade each other using information and facts and try to reach a consensus on issues. It is not uncommon for two or more administrators to trade off resources to make their respective buildings more productive. Between more senior and newer administrators, the expert model of persuasion is often used.

Personal Needs

The needs of the administrator are another factor in determining which persuasion model is chosen. After a raucous faculty meeting, the administrator may feel the need to be more assertive and take control of the process for awhile. A principal who does not have tenure may not wish to be persuading with the sanction or directive model. The need for power and self-esteem enter into the process also. There will be a more detailed discussion of the personal need factor in Chapter Two.

WHERE DO WE GO FROM HERE?

Over the past several years, conflict resolution theory has developed some general beliefs. First, what may seem to be random, chaotic events are, in fact, well-organized, patterned processes. Second, although it is virtually impossible for any one person to grasp and handle all the elements involved in a conflict, it *is* possible to become skilled in procedures that will facilitate the management of conflict resolution. If administrators apply what is known about conflict, they will be able help conflicts reach a positive settlement. A school administrator should be skilled in a wide range of conflict management techniques, because no one model will work in every case.

Of all the persuasion models, the developer model has the potential to lead to the most effective, long-lasting change. All the other models are less desirable because they call for one or more of the parties to give up or lose something as part of the settlement or change process. Only the developer model makes it possible for all parties involved in the conflict to gain something. The opportunity for positive growth and change in a school rests more clearly with the developer model than with any other. Because the developer model is the least well known among school administrators, it is the one process of conflict resolution that will be discussed in detail in the next three chapters.

SUMMARY

This chapter focused on the nature of conflict and the nature of power as they relate to the school administrator. Both conflict and power were seen as processes involving a series of events that are patterned and ordered. Sources of conflict in education were discussed, as were the three different types of conflict found in schools. Three specific phases of conflict were described—the smoke, the fire, and the ashes. Methods of dealing with conflict before it erupts into a full confrontation were discussed. Sources of power were identified as well as the functional quality of power to create change, Of the different bases of power, the two most significant—the ability to effect the right decisions and the ability to persuade—were described in detail.

The school administrator is seen as a manager who makes decisions while implementing change. Because of this need to make critical decisions on the run, the administrator is open to bias in decision making. Four different forms of bias that the administrator should avoid were illustrated. As a persuader, the school administrator uses five different models: sanction, directive, bargaining, expert advice, and developer. The choice of model depends on factors such as time, objectives, and who is involved. These five persuasion models were discussed individually and compared. The developer model of persuasion was recommended as being the most helpful in conflict management.

SUGGESTED READINGS

Argyris, Christopher. (1970). *Intervention Theory and Method.* Reading, MA: Addison-Wesley.

Cohen, Herb. (1980). *You Can Negotiate Anything.* New York: Bantam.

Conklin, Robert. (1979). *How to Get People to Do Things.* New York: Ballantine.

Jandt, Fred E. (1985). *Win–Win Negotiating: Turning Conflict into Agreement.* New York: Wiley.

Matteson, Michael T., Ivancevich, John M. (1987). *Controlling Work Stress.* San Francisco: Jossey-Bass.

Peters, Tom. (1987). *Thriving on Chaos.* New York: Knopf.

Raiffa, Howard. (1982). *The Art and Science of Negotiation.* Cambridge, MA: Harvard University Press.

Tjosvold, Dean. (1984). "Effects of Crisis Orientation on Managers' Approach to Controversy in Decision Making." *Academy of Management Journal. 27,* 130–138.

Wales, Charles E.; Nardi, Anne H.; & Stager, Roger A. (1986). "Decision Making: A New Paradigm for Education." *Educational Leadership, 43* (May), 37–41.

CONFLICT RESOLUTION GUIDE

Each chapter in this book contains a Conflict Resolution Guide. You can use this guide as a worksheet for any ongoing conflict resolutions in which you are involved. It can serve as a checklist for determining where you are in the resolution process and where you need to go.

1. In the present conflict, determine the source of the disagreement. Is it conflicting or ambiguous roles, interests, communication, consensus, rules, or prior conflicts?

   _____

   _____

   _____

2. Determine the type of conflict.

   Type I: Incompatible goals

   _____

   Type II: Parties want different things but must settle
   on one solution.

   _____

   Type III: Parties want the same thing but only one can
   have it.

   _____

3. At what stage is the conflict?

   Smoke _____

   Fire_____

   Ashes _____

4. How does your decision measure up to this standard?

   The right policy with observable action goals

   _____

   _____

   _____

   _____

   _____

5. At this point in your decision making, can you detect any bias on your part? Is there bias based on overconfidence, negative perception of risk, or personality?

_____

_____

_____

_____

6. What model of persuasion have you chosen and why?

Sanction _____

Directive _____

Bargaining _____

Expert advice _____

Developer _____

7. Which factors influenced your choice of persuasion model? Was it time, objectives, roles, costs, peer group, personal need or a combination of the above? _____

_____

_____

_____

_____

CHAPTER TWO

Preparing for Confrontation

Is the process of moving toward resolving a conflict really a process of preparing for confrontation? The answer is yes if you are referring to the need to marshal all your resources—your creativity, your wits, and your ability to relate positively to people to focus on the presenting problem. But the answer is no if you are expecting to see a winner and a loser in the aftermath of the conflict. Resolution is a process that employs tactics, offers, counteroffers, and more tactics, and which finally culminates in some sort of settlement. The conflict resolution process is dynamic, energized, confusing, and sometimes full of tension. The participants are often torn between trying to get what they want and trying to understand what the other side wants. This chapter will address the steps the participants need to take before resolving a conflict. A good proportion of the gains you may want to capture in the settlement will be identified in this preparation process.

The specific techniques described here include ways of assessing the climate or the ethos of the conflict, assessing your role and purpose, determining your alternatives, planning the meeting's agenda, and uncovering any hidden agendas that might exist. Remember that there are both formal and informal conflict resolution processes. Whether you are preparing to sit down at a table with others to discuss the conflict (formal) or have been approached in the school corridors by someone with a conflict (informal), you can use the techniques described here to help set the stage for a successful settlement.

To facilitate your understanding of how to use these techniques, a specific example will be described throughout this book. You will be able to see how a conflict moves toward settlement as it proceeds through each of the stages of the conflict resolution process. Although the principal is sometimes one of the parties to a conflict, in this example the principal plays the role of a mediator between two disputants. As you read this case, you may find that some of the methods used by the principal do not seem appropriate or are not ones that you would use. This example is not meant to show *the* way to resolve a dispute. Rather, it demonstrates how one school administrator tried to resolve a serious conflict using some of the skills described in these chapters. A brief background of the conflict is given here.

MICHAEL'S CONFLICT

Michael's parents, Mr. and Mrs. James, came to the principal two weeks before the first quarter began. Their complaint was that the English teacher, Mr. Fritz, was failing to understand Michael's learning problems. Their complaint centered on an assigned book report that was beyond Michael's academic ability to complete. They demanded that Michael be removed from the class and be reassigned to another English teacher.

The principal had the school's guidance counselor arrange a meeting with the English teacher, Michael, and his parents to determine the issues involved and possibly reach a settlement. But the counselor reported to the principal that the meeting had been a disaster. The teacher accused Michael of laziness, and the parents accused the teacher of bigotry. At this point, the parents were refusing to have their son return to the class. They demanded that his class assignment be changed.

Now, the principal had to meet with all the disputants and try to reach a mutually agreeable resolution. Before the meeting could take place, however, the English teacher informed Michael that his English grade for the first quarter had been recorded as an F. Michael's parents responded that they were going to write a letter to the board of education if their demands were not met.

SETTING A POSITIVE CLIMATE

Four factors must be present for the participants in any conflict to have a chance to reach a successful settlement. These factors provide the positive climate or ethos that allows a mutually agreeable solution to be determined. They are:

• Absence of a power struggle
• Presence of high stakes
• Presence of a working relationship
• Presence of an ability to engage in joint problem solving

Each of these factors will be explored further here.

Absence of a Power Struggle

The idea of *power* is attractive to most people. We all want some degree of power, and we all want to avoid being under someone else's power. Power can be both good and bad. Some people define all of life as a game of power; the goal is to know what you want and use power to get it. Others feel that power is inherently destructive and that using it is immoral. Completing Activity 2-1 will help you understand your own use of power.

Power that is directed toward dominating or manipulating others is the type of power that is destructive. Most people in conflict resolution situations have experienced power as either the dominator—the winner—or as the submissive party—the loser. Few experiences in our lives present us with alternatives to conflict resolution other than being either a winner or a loser. Those in a position of authority often come to conflict resolution meetings seeking, with the best of intentions, to impose a settlement. Their method is one of *imposition* rather than *exposition* of a solution. Such people deprive others of their right and responsibility to become involved in problem solving.

When one participant tries to manipulate or dominate negotiations, one of four things can happen. The first possibility is that you give in and allow the other person to impose the solution. Then he or she wins and you lose. As a second alternative, you may not give in but may, in turn, manage to impose your solution. In this case you win and the other person loses. In both of these two situations you will probably end up with a solution that has little if any chance of working for long. Whoever wins, you will distance your-

___ **ACTIVITY 2-1** _____

Listed here are a number of questions related to power. After each question, circle your response.

1. Do you feel that the best solution to a problem is one that is imposed?

                                                          YES   NO

2. Do you formulate a plan of action that includes the ways people will think and feel about your solution?

                                                          YES   NO

3. Do your teachers and other staff members think of you as a team player?

                                                          YES   NO

4. Do you include as many people as possible who are affected by the problem in the process of seeking a solution?

                                                          YES   NO

5. When you receive a complaint, do you act on it immediately, before gathering information?

                                                          YES   NO

If you answered NO, YES, YES, YES, and NO, in that order, you can consider yourself a successful mover of power. If you have more than one "incorrect" answer, you probably find yourself involved in many power struggles as you negotiate. Implementing the tactics described in the next few chapters will help you avoid these unnecessary and costly power struggles.

self from your opponent and destroy all possibility of mutually resolving any future conflicts.

A third alternative is that you recognize the emerging power struggle, decide to avoid it altogether, and simply walk out. In this case you may have won, but the problem still exists, waiting for a solution. The fourth alternative is for you to recognize the power struggle for what it is, share your perceptions with the other participant, and decide to drop the struggle and move on to solve the problem.

How do you move on? You do not do it by imposing power. Rather, you adopt the developer model, described in Chapter One.

Assuming here that you are the one in authority and therefore the one in the position of power, you decide to give up your power and invite the other person to become a participant in searching for the solution. The solution is simple: Give up your power! "What!" you may say. "Give up my power? Are you crazy? I'm sure to be destroyed!" Not so. The dynamics of power are paradoxical. The more power you give up, the more power comes back to you. That may sound irrational, but it is true.

The best run multinational corporations are doing just this (John Hoerr, "The Payoff from Teamwork," *Business Week*, July 10, 1989, pp. 54–62). Power is being surrendered. The central corporate headquarters are being reduced in size in favor of delegating authority to the regional and divisional levels. Power has been given out to those who need it to compete in solving the problems of today's business world. What is happening back at corporate headquarters? Problems are being solved at the local level faster and with less conflict, and the results are being seen in high productivity, increases in sales, and high staff morale.

Power struggles lead to no lasting gains. Someone wins, but usually not for long. The conflict simmers and resurfaces later with another issue. Problem solving is based on trust, communication, respect, and participation, not on the use of power to get your own way.

What do you do if the other person will not give up the power struggle, even after you have gone to great lengths to make everyone aware that it exists? What do you do if you are willing to invoke a participatory developer model, but the other person wants to impose a solution? In that situation, read the section of Chapter Six on how to deal with game playing in power struggles. Remember, the power struggle must end for a solution to be reached.

Presence of High Stakes

The various participants must have enough energy to move the resolution toward settlement. This can only come from the personal investment of the participants. People will only involve themselves in something that is worth the effort. Therefore, the stakes need to be relatively high for all participants.

As a school administrator, you cannot get involved in every conflict that comes through your office door. You need to set priorities. You must deal with those conflicts that cannot tolerate a mistake. Other, less crucial conflicts can be delegated to others who are closer to the action. Activity 2-2 will help you rank your conflicts.

In our case example of Michael's conflict, the principal initially decided to delegate the conflict between the English teacher and the parents to the guidance counselor. He judged correctly that the counselor would be in a better position to collect the facts, assess the situation, and facilitate the discussion because the counselor already had a working relationship with the parents, Michael, and the teacher involved. The failure of the discussion to settle anything is not as disastrous as it may seem. The fact that the principal could delegate the responsibility of settlement to the counselor was worth the risk involved.

Delegation does not mean that administrators give up their responsibility but, rather, that they share this responsibility with others. It is a measure of their respect for and confidence in the person to whom they delegate the conflict resolution. With guided experience, training, and supervision, others can handle the process as well or better. Administrators should always consider delegating conflicts that are routine, time-consuming, or part of a larger conflict resolution process.

Presence of a Working Relationship

The two parties to any dispute need to build a relationship if any meaningful negotiations are to take place. In some cases this relationship may already exist. But if the parties are new to each other, or if there is a history of negative feelings, the following suggestions may help them build a working relationship.

- Listen more than you talk:
  Do not finish another person's sentence.
  Do not interrupt another person's apology.
- When you do talk:
  Give opinions.
  Ask questions.
  Admit misunderstandings.
- Show enthusiasm:
  Take time to understand.
  Go to lunch or break with another person.
  Show a smile.
  Give a handshake.
  Be assertive in your voice.

┌───┐

ACTIVITY 2-2

To determine your priorities, you may need to complete the rank-ordering that follows.

   Step 1: List all the things you did yesterday on the job. Divide the items on this list into categories, such as scheduling, disciplining, monitoring, conducting, supervising, visiting, and meeting. Brainstorm these activities with others in your office. There are probably many more than you can think of. Then list them here.

_____

_____

_____

_____

_____

   Step 2: As you look over this list, choose the five activities that you consider most important. Rank-order them here from the most important (in your view) to least important.

1. _____

2. _____

3. _____

4. _____

5. _____

   Step 3: For the remaining activities, list those you feel are the least important to your job as a school administrator:

1. _____

2. _____

3. _____

4. _____

5. _____

   Now that you have identified the least important activities, consider delegating them. There is no need to waste your energies on such activities if someone else can handle them. Save yourself for those activities that have the highest stakes involved. The following is a typical delegation chart:

└───┘

Date	Activity	Due Date	Date In	Remarks

- Show encouragement:
  Share your vision.
  Demonstrate a can-do approach.
  Celebrate the small steps.
  Stress the skills of everyone involved.
- Be honest:
  Admit problems.
  Express, but do not demonstrate, your feelings.
  Share some personal information about yourself.

Presence of an Ability to Engage in Joint Problem Solving

You should determine whether all parties to the conflict resolution process have the authority to solve the problem and reach a settlement. If any one of the parties is not in a position to make a decision about the issue, you should lower your expectations of this negotiation. Often your role or that of another party may be primarily to share information or exchange ideas, because you do not have the direct authority to make a formal settlement. If this is the case, your role should be made clear from the outset. A simple question can give you the information you need: "Do you have the authority in this situation to settle this problem?" If the answer is yes, you can proceed. If the answer is no, you need to ask one of these two questions: "What can you offer me now in this talk?" or "Whom do I have to go to in order to reach someone who *can* make a decision on this issue?"

If you are negotiating with a group or if two groups of individuals represent the parties in a negotiation, the question of who has the authority to solve the problem is more challenging. Group behavior is a complex process, which goes beyond the scope of this chapter. Some of the references at the end of this chapter can provide a greater understanding of group process.

A group has three essential functions:

1. Moving toward or away from establishing its identity
2. Maintaining its identity
3. Transforming its identity

Throughout these sets of functions, a group is also trying to accomplish a task by mobilizing its resources and trying to stabilize internal conflicts among its members. To understand what a group is all about, picture a faculty meeting at the end of a school day. The principal usually is trying to move through the agenda and accomplish the task, while some individual staff members are talking in small groups at their tables about disagreements concerning the school. This is an example of the task versus the social dynamics of the group.

To apply this to decision-making processes, a group needs to be able to overcome obstacles to communication among its members if it is to achieve and validate a consensus. To accomplish this, groups usually need a number of individuals who are called *unconflicted persons*—individuals who can make objective judgments, lack compulsiveness, and are not disillusioned with the leader. These are the people to look for in preliminary discussions with the group. If you can find them among the group members, you can be relatively confident that this group will be able to overcome any natural tendency to collapse under its internal conflicts and be unable to reach consensus. Completing Activity 2-3 will help you identify staff members who can influence a group.

PREPARATION

About half of all negotiation takes place in the preparation. There is no substitute for a good preparation strategy. Just as a good classroom teacher always prepares, so, too, a good administrator takes the time to plan the conflict resolution process. Those who tell you that they "just wing it" are usually poor negotiators. This section deals with five areas that call for careful planning.

What Is the Purpose?

The purpose of negotiation is either to identify a problem, to solve a problem, or to refine a settlement. Often, participants come to a meeting with different purposes, and the initial discussion results in confusion and backtracking to sort out everyone's intent. To avoid this, be clear from the beginning about the purpose of the

---

ACTIVITY 2-3

Consider the staff members with whom you have regular contact, and decide which of them have the following characteristics.

1. Ability to make independent judgments

_____

_____

_____

2. Ability to avoid compulsiveness

_____

_____

_____

3. Ability to avoid conflict with the leader (whoever the leader may be in relation to that person, for example the union chief, principal, or superintendent)

_____

_____

_____

   Any individual who meets two of these three criteria is a prime mover who can influence a group. A person who fits all three criteria is a powerful potential ally. Such a person needs to be nurtured, and his or her advice should be sought.

---

meeting. Convey your intent to the other parties before you meet, and reiterate your intent at the onset of the exchange.

MICHAEL'S CONFLICT

In the case of Michael and the principal, each party brought a different purpose to the meeting. The parents wanted the meeting to make a change in the English teacher, the teacher wanted to vindicate his actions and prove the justice of his position, and the counselor was looking for a peaceful end to a confrontation she felt she had been unable to control. Everyone wanted to solve a problem, but, each had a different problem in mind. The principal's intent was different. He saw the purpose of the meeting as not to solve a problem but, rather, to identify the problem for all concerned and to preserve the policies of the school. He was looking at all the facts and asking the participants to identify the major issues at the center of the dispute. There will be a fuller discussion of this in the section of the next chapter dealing with Tactic 1.

What Is Your Role?

Although a school administrator can be one of the disputants in a conflict, very often the role thrust upon the administrator is that of mediator. Parents, students, teachers, and other administrators all look to the administrator to mediate disputes. It is not inconceivable that the administrator will have two roles to occupy in a given situation—that of disputant and that of mediator.

This is illustrated by the case in which two teachers come to the superintendent to complain about the behavior of a principal when, as it happens, the superintendent was the authority who directed the principal to perform the action that prompted the complaint. The superintendent must walk a tightrope, mediating the dispute while at the same time being one of the parties to it. To do this, the superintendent must be able to keep both roles clearly in mind.

Part of the process of identifying your role is determining what you think would be a good settlement option for you and for the other participants involved. What would you like to see happen? Having a clear expectation of the outcome is essential in reaching a goal.

MICHAEL'S CONFLICT

In Michael's case, the principal clearly did not want the parents to write a letter of complaint to the board of education. He also wanted to preserve the school's grading process. Once a teacher had given a grade, the principal did not want to change that grade. The principal guessed that the parents wanted to have the F grade dropped and the English teacher changed. The teacher wanted the F to remain and wanted to keep the student in the class; he felt that for Michael to leave would be taking the easy way out, and that would not help the boy later in life.

No matter what role or expectation the administrator has chosen or has been thrust into, his or her trustworthiness needs to be clearly established. If the participants do not trust the administrator, attempts to resolve the conflict will be fraught with obstacles. *Trust* in this context means that the participants must see the administrator as possessing truth, wisdom, and integrity.

Truth

The administrator must have the ability to disseminate valid, reliable information to all parties involved. Do the participants believe that information coming from the administrator is accurate? Does this information remain constant over time, or does it change to fit the administrator's needs? In resolving a dispute, certain critical facts of the case are needed. Usually the school administrator either knows them or has the resources to obtain them. If the other participants doubt the validity of these facts, then the process is in jeopardy from the beginning.

An example from one school district in the Midwest illustrates how information with a twist of humor can disarm a conflict situation before the storm gathers. It has always been custom at this district to pay the teaching staff on the Wednesday before Thanksgiving. Regular payday would have fallen on the Friday, but because the schools were closed teachers received their pay early. One year the teachers waited all day Wednesday for their checks, but the checks did not come. The superintendent of schools sent this message to the staff.

EXAMPLE

To Staff:
Last Wednesday I know all of you expected to be paid, as has been our custom for many years. The reason you had to receive the checks in the mail on Friday and Saturday was the result of a number of factors.

When the school district's checks came into my office from the regional processing center, they were posted with the wrong date—Friday's date, not Wednesday's. If we issued these checks, you would not have been able to cash them until Friday. I made a decision to return the checks to the center when they promised me they could issue a new set before the schools were dismissed for the day. At noon I was informed the correct checks were ready and the driver we had waiting for them started to return to the district. The district car he was driving broke down. At 1:30 P.M. I sent another driver to get the checks. This driver got lost on the way and could not find the broken-down car. By the time the checks were finally delivered to my office, it was 4:00 P.M. All of you had left for the Thanksgiving weekend. I held the business office personnel on overtime and we mailed the checks to you. Those of you in town received your checks on Friday, and the others got them the next day, Saturday.

I apologize for the stress and inconvenience caused to our teachers. I hope we were the only inedible turkeys in your holiday weekend.

Wisdom

School administrators display wisdom when they demonstrate a grasp of the major issues of the conflict and a positive attitude of expectancy. They are able to transcend the minute details of the conflict, to avoid becoming embroiled in the personality clashes of the participants, and to keep their own egos out of the conflict. They are able, as James MacGregor Burns noted in *Leadership* (New York: Harper & Row, 1978), to mobilize, in competition or conflict with others, institutional, political, psychological, and other resources sufficient to arouse, engage, and satisfy the motives of others.

Wise administrators avoid wielding naked power but are able to raise the participants to higher levels of motivation and even of morality. Throughout the conflict resolution process, they are able to build and maintain the four basic human needs of the school's organization:

1. People's need for meaning
2. People's need for a modicum of control
3. People's need to think of themselves as winners
4. The understanding that actions and behaviors shape attitudes and beliefs rather than vice versa

For more discussion of this topic, see *In Search of Excellence* by Thomas J. Peters and Robert H. Waterman (New York: Harper & Row, 1982).

With wisdom, the administrator can foster the building of coalitions among school personnel to get things done. This can be a frustrating, time-consuming process. It demands that the administrator get involved in team building, be tough when necessary in order to make decisions, be able to listen, be visible, and be able to change the school's structure to facilitate collaborative management. Administrators are the ones who can shift the structure of the school and mobilize individuals to move into action rapidly if necessary to reach a conflict settlement. They are known to follow up frequently and swiftly on settlement implementation. There is an air of expectancy when such administrators are asked to enter into the conflict resolution process because the participants know that the problem will be acted on, that something will happen fairly quickly, and that this action will be meaningful and satisfying to all involved.

Activity 2-4 provides you with a scale for measuring your own skills in handling conflict management.

Integrity

Administrators with integrity are people who are driven by a vision of what they think the business of education is all about. They place a very high priority on education—that is, on teaching and

---

ACTIVITY 2-4

In the course of reading this book, you will learn a great many skills and be exposed to a broad range of conflict management ideas. How you use this knowledge base is a measure of your wisdom. Now, take a minute to measure your level of skill in handling conflict in your job.

The following scale goes from 1 to 10, with 10 representing the highest or most skilled level of conflict management. Level 5 would be considered an average level of skill. Level 1 represents the bottom—no known ability to manage conflict. Where would you rate yourself? Circle your skill number.

10	9	8	7	6	5	4	3	2	1

Highest	Average	Low
skill level	skill level	skill level

At the end of this book you will be asked to return to this scale and rate yourself again on your level of skill in implementing conflict management techniques. You will then have a basis for comparison.

learning. The other functions of the school—custodial care, sorting, and evaluating—are considered secondary goals in relation to the school's primary mission. Administrators with integrity are seen by others as not only supporting this mission but also being able to communicate it.

In conflict situations these administrators will make decisions on the basis of the values inherent in the mission statement. There is a congruence in their thinking, as everything related to the school revolves around the primary mission. Such people have a perspective that transcends mundane conflicts. By taking this broader view, they are able to take time to think and analyze decisions as they relate to the mission statement's values.

These people are persistent in holding out for a decision based on the stated mission values. The other parties involved in a dispute with such people can guess what their decision will be on issues that are clear-cut. For more complicated issues, the parties can be assured that no judgment will occur before the matter is reconciled with the administrator's values. Astute participants will try to present their arguments for a particular decision in a light favorable to the administrator's stated values. They also know that such administrators are savvy enough to realize that this is happening and that they will still base their decisions on a thorough comparison of the conflict's facts and the school's mission values.

Integrity is not a quality a new administrator can impose. It takes years to establish among staff members. It evolves over time as their trust in the administrator develops. What is surprising and reassuring is that once the integrity is established, the administrator is allowed to make mistakes. Staff members do not become overly concerned when the administrator makes a mistake because they know that he or she based the decision on a judgment process grounded in honesty, and fundamental values. Mistakes can be corrected, and the understanding that everyone is human gives administrators the freedom to judge issues on the basis of their integrity.

See the end of Chapter Six for an activity that can help you in developing your own mission statement.

What Is Your BATNA?

The acronym BATNA stands for "best alternative to a negotiated agreement." A BATNA is a plan or series of strategies you have devised for securing your interests if the present negotiation does not reach a successful settlement. It is the point in the negotiation process at which you feel that your best gain will come if no agreement is reached at all—the point at which it is to your advantage just to walk away.

Conflict resolution is designed to produce an agreement that is better than the results you can achieve without negotiating and better than your present situation. Yet you need a standard by which to measure the various options of settlement. The only way to know that the settlement option is better than what you have now or what you could get if you walk away is to develop your BATNA. Many participants rush to settlement because they are pessimistic about the consequences of not reaching an agreement. They have no flexibility in generating alternatives to settlement because they have no way to measure how the various options would affect their choice of the ultimate option—walking away.

In every negotiation process you fear that you may accept an apparently favorable settlement option that later, in hindsight, does not look like such a good deal. To protect yourself, you need to develop a bottom line. This is the point beyond which you will never go in negotiation. It is the same as saying to a tag sale dealer, "I'll offer you $20, no more, for that stereo." If the dealer wants more than that, you will walk away without the stereo. You and the dealer both lose.

In the case of Michael, the principal might say to himself:

Look, I would rather not change the student's grade or his teacher. Yet I understand these parents are going to persist. Therefore, my bottom line in this meeting is that if I cannot convince them to leave things as they are, then I will allow Michael to retake the quarter exam to see if he can get a better grade. If the parents do not meet my demand, then I will leave things as they are.

Failure to resolve this problem will be the result if the parents refuse to accept the principal's bottom-line offer. Then, they will indeed walk away and will probably make good their threat to go the board of education.

Having a bottom-line strategy limits you in your negotiation. Once the negotiation reaches the subjective line you have established, you should walk away. Then, however, you are left with your interest or need unfulfilled. Bottom lines are therefore limiting and can be dangerous in planning negotiations. You are in a much stronger position in negotiating if you have developed a BATNA that you can implement without having to walk away. You need to be imaginative enough to generate a host of settlement options while remaining secure in the knowledge that you have a way out if the options being offered seem to give you no more than you already have. Before you enter the negotiation process, you will need to develop your BATNA. The process involves three steps, which were expressed in "The Theory and Practice of Negotiation," a lecture by Lawrence Susskind at the 1987 Summer Institute on The Principal and School Improvement, at Harvard University.

1. List all the actions you could *possibly* take if no agreement is reached. Make use of all your resources—time, imagination, people, and money.
2. Develop action steps to convert the ideas developed in the previous step into specific, concrete alternatives. The format should be: Who is going to do What, and When.
3. Choose the one alternative developed in the previous step that looks most promising and also satisfies you the most.

MICHAEL'S CONFLICT

In Michael's case the principal developed a number of alternatives to agreement, as follows:

Listen to all sides of the dispute and decide that more time is needed to make a decision. Arrange another meeting.

Provide an educational evaluation for Michael to determine his academic strengths and weaknesses.

Assign a learning disability specialist or tutor to Michael to help him through the English course.

Convince the English teacher that having Michael in his class will only intensify his confrontation with the parents.

Ask the teacher to throw Michael out of the class.

Ask the counselor to help Michael assert himself and declare his wishes in the process. Possibly the parties would listen to Michael more readily than they will to each other.

The principal decided his best option was the first on the list—to work for more time. He felt that more time was to his advantage. If Michael had to stay in the class, both the teacher and the parents would become restless and might yield somewhat in their demands. The principal guessed that neither party wanted the confrontation to escalate and that both parties wanted a quick solution.

Another preparation in the development of a BATNA is to try to guess what the other party's BATNA may be. If you can guess correctly or even try to have others reveal their BATNA in prenegotiation talks, you have a distinct advantage. If their BATNA is powerful and you really want to reach a successful agreement, you may need to help them lower their expectations of achieving their BATNA.

Activity 2-5 gives you an opportunity to develop your own BATNA for a particular conflict.

MICHAEL'S CONFLICT

In our case the principal knew that the BATNA of the parents was the option of going to the board of education. In fact, they told him that was their intention. If the parents felt that they were not going to reach a settlement they liked, they would simply walk away from the talks and go over the principal's head. The principal guessed, on the basis of his knowledge of the English teacher's past behavior, that the teacher would most likely appeal his case to the chairman of the English department, who was a close personal friend of the principal. The English teacher would calculate that this friend would persuade the principal to give in to the teacher's demands.

In making these guesses, the principal also guessed that for political reasons neither party wanted to invoke its BATNA too quickly, and that time was a factor he could manipulate in trying to have the parties reach a successful settlement.

DETERMINING THE AGENDA

You can approach the conflict resolution meeting with a number of different agendas. The more common ones are described in this section. For further reading in this area, see David A. Lax and James K. Sebenius. *The Manager as Negotiator* (New York: Free Press, 1986, p. 68). You should consider how you would like to organize the meeting. Sometimes you have no choice because the conflict is thrust upon you with no time to prepare, but more often

---

ACTIVITY 2-5

Provided here is an opportunity for you to develop your own BATNAs for a particular conflict you may be dealing with.

BATNA Development Chart

Step 1. List every possible alternative to agreement.

_____

_____

_____

_____

Step 2. Action plan for these alternatives:

Alternative 1	Who	What	When

_____

_____

Alternative 2	Who	What	When

_____

_____

Alternative 3	Who	What	When

_____

_____

Step 3: Best alternative

_____

_____

_____

Ways to improve this choice:

_____

_____

Ways it is most satisfying:

_____

than not there is a great deal of latitude in how to organize the meeting.

Single Issue

Here, one issue is brought to the table and is the only issue discussed. For example, suppose a teacher asks the superintendent of schools to grant her an additional personal day because she was in an accident on the way to school but had no more sick or personal days left according to the contract. In this case there is only one issue before the superintendent. He can decide it on its own merits, without any other issues complicating the decision making.

This single-issue agenda is useful when there is a lack of time, energy, or the right people to produce a more complicated settlement. Its disadvantage is the failure to link issues and the lack of collaborative problem solving. This agenda also can break down quickly. For example, suppose a shop teacher tells a parent that his son has to stay after school for detention. The father says his son will stay after school only if he can use the time to make up missed work. The teacher agrees but insists that it is detention even though the student will be able to complete his missed work. The father wants his son to complete the work but does not want him to stay after school because the teacher is calling it detention. This conflict quickly reaches an impasse because the disputants have entered the resolution process using a single-issue approach. If they used a different organizational approach, they might well reach a mutually agreeable settlement.

Many administrators use the single-issue approach because it is quick and easy, and it can be quite satisfactory. Other administrators use this approach to open a Pandora's box. They use the single issue as a link to other issues or to package a settlement that is favorable to everyone involved.

Easy Ones First

Few building-level school administrators have time for this approach. It requires that the parties choose the least conflict-provoking issues to settle first and then move on to issues where there are more areas of disagreement. A list of the issues is developed beforehand and rank-ordered by degree of difficulty. The approach can be very effective, especially for parties who are new to each other. But the formality of this approach is something that most building-level personnel would find contrived.

The advantage of this agenda is that it promotes the habit of agreement. The easy issues are usually agreed on quickly, a positive attitude is created, and terms and possible issues are defined. Also, as the negotiations move on to the more difficult issues, the parties are reluctant to walk out because some issues have already reached settlement, and these gains are not easily given up.

The disadvantage of this agenda is that it generally relies on a formal agreement in advance among the parties as to which issues will be discussed early on and which are more difficult and should wait. This process is a negotiation in and of itself. Again, it can be accomplished in a formal setting or an informal one, depending on the skill of the administrator.

Another disadvantage of this approach is that there is little linking of issues. Once an issue has been settled, there is no way to return to it and tie it to another issue.

As an example, take the case of the superintendent of schools and the teachers' union president who decide to talk about a list of minor grievances from the various teacher units in the district. First, the superintendent and the union president rank-ordered their respective issues according to how easily they think the issues will be to settle. They then compare notes and make a joint list, which they then move through item by item. The teachers' desire for more parking spaces might be easily resolved, for example, if the superintendent agrees to open the lower field to the teachers' cars. The union president in turn might agree with the superintendent's wish that the final June paycheck be distributed in three payments rather than the normal two payments.

Principles

Participants with this type of agenda agree to negotiate at a higher or more abstract level of principles. They agree to defer decisions on specific issues until they reach a clarification and settlement on the principles involved in the negotiation. The application of these principles to the specific issues then becomes the substance of the negotiation.

The advantage of this agenda is that the minor issues are bypassed temporarily. Expanding the negotiation in this way opens up the settlement possibilities beyond the narrow range offered in the single-issue approach. It is more likely that both parties to the dispute will gain from the process rather than each party either winning or losing. The disadvantage is that the parties have to disengage themselves from their single-issue approach and be willing to look at the larger principles on which the single issue rests. This involves more risk, usually more time, and definitely more cooperation among the participants. For an example, let us look at our case study of Michael's conflict.

MICHAEL'S CONFLICT

In the case of Michael, the principal decided earlier that he had the time to negotiate a more comprehensive settlement. Therefore, he decided to try to get both parties, the teacher and the parents, to agree to look at some of the larger principles involved in the dispute. The parents saw the problem as that of a bigoted teacher who did not understand or care about their son's learning problems. The teacher saw the dispute as a violation of his professional judgment and, indeed, his right to grade as he saw fit. The principal, however, saw the issue differently. He took a broader approach, which temporarily put both opposing views aside and highlighted issues of the school's due process in evaluating students and the students' need to learn the concepts involved in this English class. In this way the issue became the two functions of the educational organization: to sort and evaluate students, and to teach and educate them.

Trade-offs

Using this agenda, the parties enter the negotiation process with the intention of making some trade-offs. Both parties expect to gain something, but they agree to base their gains on the reciprocal action of the other party.

The advantage of using this type of agenda is that all the issues are discussed simultaneously, rather than one by one. The issues are looked at as a whole; and, as trade-offs are made, they are gradually eliminated. The chief disadvantage of this approach is that one of the parties may view the trade-off as being forced. They are not really willing to give in on the issue but feel it is the only way to gain something else. Their initial lack of commitment may lead to problems in sustaining the settlement later on.

An example of this is seen in the case of parents who approached the local district committee on special education to demand that the director of special services change their son's designated counselor to another individual on staff. The counselor assigned to the boy saw the boy as manipulating his parents in his effort to change counselors because the boy was uncomfortable with the counselor's attempts to implement behavior change strategies. This boy, the counselor said, was a master manipulator. He wanted his parents to make this demand because he did not want to work during the counseling sessions at changing his behavior. In fact, the counselor wanted to have the boy transferred to a group situation where his peers could help him develop more responsible behavior. Up to now, however, the parents had refused this request.

The settlement reached during the negotiation was a trade-off. The boy would be transferred to another counselor for individual sessions related to improving classroom work, but he would also be required to start group counseling work with the original counselor. The focus of this group would be on implementing behavioral change strategies for social problems.

Which to Use?

Finding the proper agenda requires some prenegotiating skill. Often the agenda is set by precedent or by the wish of the more powerful of the two parties. One principal, trying to have his district upgrade the science labs, approached the budget hearing process using a principled approach. She was convinced that the need for students to have modern science equipment was basic. At the budget hearing, however, the school board made it clear that they were using a trade-off agenda. The principal could have her new science equipment only if she was willing to give up two math periods so that a math teacher could be transferred to the junior high school. Needless to say, the principal switched her agenda and started to negotiate the school's budget using a trade-off agenda.

Other issues to consider are how much time, energy, and human resources you are willing to commit to the resolution process. Figure 2-1 presents a comparison of the different agendas with regard to these issues. Completing Activity 2-6 will help you determine which agenda is appropriate.

As you move from left to right, the amount of time, energy, and people involved in the conflict resolution process increases.

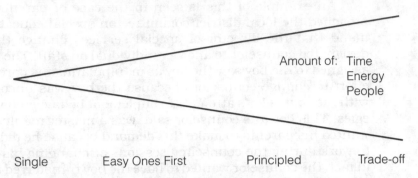

Amount of: Time
            Energy
            People

Single   Easy Ones First   Principled   Trade-off

Figure 2-1. Comparison of Conflict Resolution Agendas

   After reflecting on your responses, choose the type of agenda you feel offers you the most advantages and the fewest advantages. Share your responses with a colleague. Did he or she choose a different agenda? If so, ask why. Does the answer force you to reconsider your response?

Uncovering Hidden Agendas

There are hidden agendas in every conflict resolution process because of the tension that exists between the participants' need to settle the conflict and their need to gain as much from the settlement as possible. The tension caused by the question, "When do I give in and when do I pressure for more concessions?" can be intense. Hidden agendas cannot be ignored or avoided. They are neither good nor bad in themselves, but you can learn to control them.
   The first step is to be aware of the factors that produce hidden agendas. Where do they come from? The three most common sources of hidden agendas are:

• Personal needs
• Political behavior
• Administrative style

This section deals with each of these sources in turn.

ACTIVITY 2-6

The following worksheet can help you determine which negotiating agenda is best. Consider one of the conflicts in which you are involved. After each negotiating agenda, list the advantages and disadvantages associated with it.

Type

1. Single-issue:

   Advantages _____

   _____

   _____

   Disadvantages _____

   _____

   _____

   _____

2. Easy ones first:

   Advantages _____

   _____

   _____

   Disadvantages _____

   _____

   _____

3. Principled:

   Advantages _____

   _____

   _____

   Disadvantages _____

   _____

   _____

4. Trade-off: _____

   Advantages _____

   _____

   _____

   Disadvantages _____

   _____

   _____

Personal Needs

All of us have an inner nature that strives to fulfill itself. It is the primary motivator of human behavior. It is unique to each person, but in general it is part of the nature of the human species. Abraham Maslow, in *Motivation and Personality* (New York: Harper & Row, 1954), describes what happens to this inner nature when it is denied its fulfillment, or what he called its *actualization*. The inner nature is not as strong as the instincts of animals. It is easily overcome by cultural and environmental pressure, by force of habit, and by a person's cognitive response to external pressures.

To understand the drives that motivate us, look at the hierarchy of needs developed by Maslow. He believed that certain basic human needs must be met before a person can be concerned with fulfilling higher level needs. This hierarchy is illustrated as a ladder (see Figure 2-2).

According to this theory, all people have these six basic needs. We all are striving to climb the ladder and reach a self-actualized state. But before we can climb the ladder, we need to satisfy our needs at each of its lower rungs. For example, people cannot be concerned with the need to be loved if they are hungry or cold. What motivates us is the desire to fulfill a particular need.

How does this theory apply to assessing hidden agendas? In a conflict resolution meeting, you can often observe personal needs surfacing. This may be subtle or it may be obvious and acknowledged. An example of an obvious hidden agenda follows:

At one board of education meeting there was debate for two hours on the special education department's budget for the

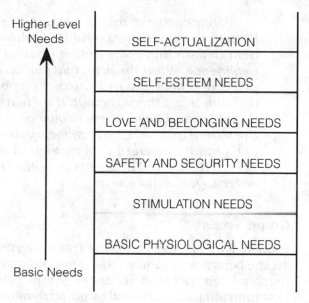

Figure 2-2. Hierarchy of Needs

next year. Most members of the board were operating from the "safety and security needs" rung of the ladder. They were trying to determine how much money the town could afford for special education. At one point, the heat in the building went off. The board members became uncomfortably cold. As the board members moved down the ladder and focused on the basic physiological needs for warmth, they quickly resolved their dispute and settled the issue simply in order to get out of the cold building. If the heat had not gone off, the dispute might not have been concluded so quickly.

Another example shows the more subtle side of hidden agendas:

After a successful high school musical performance, the principal received a letter of complaint from one of the parents who had been in the audience. The letter criticized the performance, especially the poor acoustics and poor crowd control during some of the vocal numbers. The principal felt that some of the points were valid and forwarded the letter to those in charge of the production with the hope that these points would be considered in planning the next year's performance.

Unbeknownst to the principal, the parent had also written to the superintendent of schools and the PTA president demanding some action against the principal for her negligence. What the principal saw as a valid attempt to improve a school program was transformed into a hidden agenda: to get the principal. It turned out that this parent's daughter had been turned down as a leading vocalist, and the parent was seeking revenge against the school. The parent's hidden agenda was motivated by his SELF-ESTEEM needs. He needed to see his daughter as the lead vocalist in order to feel self-esteem.

Group Needs

Hidden agendas also can come from the effect of group dynamics on the behavior of individuals. This is usually related to the interpersonal behavior that occurs in groups. This section will look at how individuals are affected by group dynamics. For more information on this topic, see *Analysis of Groups,* edited by Graham S. Gibbard, John J. Hartman, and Richard D. Mann (San Francisco: Jossey-Bass, 1976).

When a group of individuals meets to resolve a problem, a group identity is fashioned. To reach a settlement, the group as a unit can do one of six things.

1. Appeal to a higher authority.
2. Problem-solve among the group members.
3. Redefine the problem.
4. Realign expectations and accountability.
5. Increase its authority and resources.
6. Develop a group fantasy or group myth.

The last step, developing a group fantasy or group myth, occurs when the active problem-solving behavior of the group is not effective. The tension in any group member concerning how much to commit to the group and how much to hold back becomes active. The person starts to question the validity of committing oneself to a group that is ineffective, but also feels guilt and depression at the prospect of leaving the group. As the disillusionment grows, the person's internal anxieties also increase and need to be dealt with.

Rather than quit the group, the person often starts to manipulate events in an attempt to bring about real change. The person begins to develop fantasies as a means of explaining this manipulation. This person does not want to know the facts. Those facts that are unavoidable are molded to fit the developing fantasy. An example would be a school board member who is frustrated with the board's inability to reach consensus on whether to grant a principal tenure. This member wants the principal out but cannot convince the others to vote that way. When some doubt arises about what has happened to the student council's pretzel money, the board member manipulates the discussion into an investigation of the integrity of the principal. What could have been handled at a building level, with the principal investigating a theft, has now become a board of education matter, with the principal under scrutiny. As the board member continues to demand that the principal be held accountable, other inconsistencies at the school are also charged against him.

Eventually, this individual's fantasy takes hold among the others, and the development of a shared group fantasy has begun. As the momentum continues, with the group still unable to resolve its conflict, this group fantasy becomes a coherent social movement, and the principal's tenure is doomed.

The political hidden agenda is in reality the process by which the group handles the development of its identity—through integration or separation. If it can do neither, tension rises and a fantasy is likely to develop. As is often the case, individuals are locked into roles that do not reflect their abilities. The group unconsciously exploits the individual, so that all that is wrong with the group process is translated into what is wrong with a particular person. Thus, a scapegoat is created, manipulated, and eventually driven away.

Administrative Needs

Administrative needs will be discussed at length in Chapter Seven, which contains a more detailed analysis of how administrative needs foster the development of certain styles of administration or management.

Here, it is important simply to realize that administrative style does reflect a hidden agenda. People come to a resolution meeting with their own style of doing things. Although the agenda may be determined beforehand, as the tension increases, previous understandings become less binding and individuals resort to familiar behaviors. They start to manage the process on the basis of their own needs. As a result, an administrative style is demonstrated, related in part to the individuals' personal needs and in part to the group's dynamics with respect to problem solving. In the following list, a particular administrative style is paired with the corresponding behavior that can surface when tension rises in the resolution process. The reason for the behavior is often hidden, but the behavior itself can be easily observed.

Style	*Behavior*
Directive	Take control, seize power.
Analytical	Move with caution, be precise.
Behavioral	Preserve the peace and good relations.
Conceptual	Be innovative and daring in your approach.

An example of an administrator with a directive style is one who, during a budget process, seeks information from the different department heads and then develops a building-level budget independently. No tasks are delegated to others; rather, the final figures are based on this administrator's decisions. In budget negotiations, such administrators will not tolerate assistants who challenge their plans or data.

An analytical administrator might approach the budget process by sending out questionnaires and detailed cost analysis summaries of the previous year's spending by the teachers. Such an administrator would ask for precise, detailed plans and figures. In negotiations, an analytical administrator would have little tolerance for ambiguity or generalizations about projected costs.

An administrator with a behavioral style might hold many committee meetings about the budget and many discussions about the needs of the school and the staff. In negotiations over the budget, such administrators would have great difficulty deciding which needs should be cut from the budget.

A conceptual administrator would probably have the staff develop two budgets—one showing their basic needs and the other a kind of wish list of projects they would like to develop. Budget negotiations would focus on how to bring new ideas to life and how to find creative funding sources. Such administrators would tolerate ambiguity and allow a wide latitude of disagreement before the final budget items are selected.

SUMMARY

This chapter focused on the preparations a school administrator must make to resolve a conflict. The first is the creation or fostering of a positive climate. A number of factors crucial to establishing such a climate were described. In preparing for the meeting, the school administrator must develop a sense of purpose, define roles, and develop a BATNA. In determining the agenda, the administrator needs to choose a strategy—single-issue, easy issues first, principled, or trade-off. The hidden agenda of a resolution meeting also needs to be assessed. The influences of personal needs, political factors, and administrative style were discussed as possible factors in hidden agendas.

MICHAEL'S CONFLICT

The climate for the resolution meeting was a positive one. All four factors were present to ensure that a successful settlement could be reached. Although there was no power struggle yet, the parties mistrusted each other. All were making mild threats to use whatever power they had to force their demands. The parents were threatening to go over the principal's head to the board of education, and the English teacher was trying to use the power he had through the grading process. The stakes were high.

Attempts to resolve this dispute with the guidance counselor were unsuccessful, and the conflict escalated. A working relationship existed between the principal and the teacher and between the principal and the parents. Therefore, the principal used this relationship to create a mediator's role for himself. He was in an ideal position to foster an environment of positive resolution. Finally, all parties involved in the dispute were present for the negotiations, so there was an ability to engage in joint problem solving.

Although the principal chose to take the role of mediator, the principal, too, had vested interests in this dispute. Thus, the mediator's role was not a clear-cut, purely objective one. In addition to being the go-between, the principal needed to protect the policies of the school during the negotiations. The principal had to be able to handle the ambiguity of the situation and determine for himself how to move the parties toward an acceptable settlement while keeping the school's interests intact.

As was mentioned, the best alternative to a negotiated agreement (BATNA) for the principal was to listen to all parties involved in the dispute and then decide that more time was needed before a decision could be given. Time was the one factor that he determined he had, whereas the parents had little time to negotiate, because as long as an impasse existed Michael would remain in Mr. Fritz's class. With time, the principal hoped that one or both of the parties might offer a concession.

The principal knew the parents' BATNA—to write to the board of education—because they announced it. Knowing this action plan was crucial to the principal's strategy. First, it allowed him to determine that he had some reasonable time to negotiate this conflict. The parents, he guessed, would not write the letter while the negotiations were going on, but they probably would write it if the negotiations broke down. Thus, he had time to negotiate. Second, knowing the parents' BATNA allowed the principal to propose the settlement option. This gave him a clear advantage, as we will see in Chapter Four in the discussion of the tactics of settlement options.

The principal opted for a principled agenda for the resolution meeting. He did this because he had enough time and could assemble all the parties together in one building, and also because that the interests of the parties were so varied and subjective that he believed a principled settlement could be generated.

In uncovering the hidden agendas, the principal made a major tactical decision. He decided not to have Mr. Fritz present in the negotiation room. Rather, he asked that Mr. Fritz be in the adjoining faculty room while the parents met with the guidance counselor and himself. The principal determined that both the teacher and the parents were involved in fulfilling their self-esteem needs in this dispute. The teacher wanted to be sure that his integrity was not harmed. The parents wanted to ensure that their son be recognized as a bright student. Both parties, in other words, had their egos involved in this dispute. There was thus the potential for a clash of wills. Rather than risk a possible escalation of the conflict, the principal asked Mr. Fritz not to attend the meeting. This was perfectly acceptable to Mr. Fritz, who did not really want to meet with the James family.

One final preparation on the part of the principal was to telephone the parents to set the time and the date and to outline to them the format of the meeting. The parents also liked the idea of Mr. Fritz being absent. Because they wanted their son removed from the class and the failing grade removed from his record, they had no use for Mr. Fritz. They believed the principal had the total power to grant their demands.

SUGGESTED READINGS

Brazerman, Max H. (1986). *Judgment in Managerial Decision Making.* New York: Wiley.

Clark, Susan, & Ross. Victor J. (1988, April). "How We Waltzed with Our Prickly School Problem." *The Executive Educator, 10,* 22.

Cox, Allan, (1984). *The Making of the Achiever.* New York: Dodd, Mead.

Fisher, Roger, & Brown, Scott. (1988). *Getting Together; Building a Relationship That Gets to Yes.* Boston: Houghton Mifflin.

Fisher, Roger, & Ury, William. (1981). *Getting to Yes: Negotiating Agreement without Giving In.* New York: Penguin.

Strauss, Anselm. (1978). *Negotiations: Varieties. Contexts, Procedures and Social Order.* San Francisco: Jossey-Bass.

Swann, William B. (1987). "Identity Negotiation: Where Two Roads Meet." *Journal of Personality and Social Psychology, 53,* 1038–1051.

Thompson, Leigh L.; Mannix, Elizabeth A.; & Brazerman, Max H. (1988). "Negotiation: Effects of Decision Rule, Agenda, and Aspiration." *Journal of Personality and Social Psychology, 54,* 86–95.

CONFLICT RESOLUTION GUIDE

Each chapter in this book contains a Conflict Resolution Guide. You can use this guide as a worksheet for any ongoing conflict resolutions in which you are involved. It can serve as a checklist for determining where you are in the resolution process and where you need to go.

1. Is the climate right to settle? Is there an absence of a power struggle and a presence of high stakes, a working relationship, and an ability to engage in joint problem solving?

   _____

   _____

   _____

2. Are you well enough prepared for the settlement meeting? What is its purpose?

   _____

   _____

   What is your role?

   _____

   _____

   What are your plans for improving your truth, wisdom, and integrity?

   _____

   _____

3. What is your BATNA (best alternative to a negotiated agreement)?

   _____

   _____

   _____

4. What type of agenda have you planned—single-issue, easy ones first, principled, or trade-off?

   _____

   _____

   _____

   _____

5. Do you see any hidden agendas? These may be based on personal needs, political behavior, or administrator style.

_____

_____

_____

CHAPTER THREE

Dealing with Demands, Anger, and Threats

When you are well prepared for a major conflict resolution meeting, there is nothing worse than to have all your plans and hopes for a quick, positive settlement blown out of the water within the first few minutes. Meetings that start with strong statements of position, in the form of demands or even threats, can quickly deteriorate into open warfare. People who come to such meetings feeling very angry can escalate the conflict to the point of no return.

This chapter will demonstrate some tactics for reducing the effects of demands, anger, and threats. These tactics, as described in the next few chapters, are skills you can use to move a conflict resolution meeting toward a successful settlement. They involve strategies for creating shared values and joint gains and then for seizing some of these newfound gains. In Chapter One, the developer model of persuasion was described as the most comprehensive, and powerful form of reaching settlement. The tactics described here are ways of implementing the developer model by expanding the values to be gained so that every participant will gain something from the settlement. This method is radically different from the negotiation position whereby if one side gains something the other must lose something, or from the position whereby both sides have to compromise and settle for less than they had hoped. The developer model's focus is on the mutual creation of gains so that every participant receives gains, some of which may not even have been considered before the negotiation process began.

The two tactics presented in this chapter, disengaging from demands and disengaging from threats, are the initial steps you would take to help other participants alter their confrontational opening remarks. Before gains can be created, everyone's interests must be explored and affirmed. If anger is a factor, it must be defused. These tactics follow the sequential process through which most negotiations move in some fashion in their initial stages.

It is not that every negotiation proceeds steadily toward a settlement; in fact, most do not. But the process of reaching a settlement is a dynamic one, involving a series of steps or stages through which one must pass. In most negotiations the participants move back and forth from one of these stages to another. For example, the participants' opening remarks might involve a demonstration of anger. Later, after the participants have moved away from their anger and are talking about settlement possibilities, anger nevertheless may surface again. At this point all the participants have to move back in the process and deal with the expression of anger.

In this chapter the case example of Michael's conflict will be continued. As you will recall, in the previous chapter the principal had prepared himself in a number of ways to meet with Michael's parents, with the English teacher, and with the guidance counselor.

TACTIC 1: DISENGAGING FROM DEMANDS

There are various methods you can use to help clarify the issues involved in a conflict. Do not assume you know them before the meeting begins. What people say is not necessarily what they mean. People tend to want what they *need*, not what they say they want.

Use these methods described here to express the positions people take in terms of their needs or interests. For example, a teacher who presents her position as a demand that her room assignment be changed may actually be expressing a need to be closer to a colleague she admires. How one gets to these needs is what Tactic 1 is all about. If the negotiation meeting starts with a demonstration of anger, you may want to use Tactic 2 to help the angry person disengage from his or her hostile opening remarks. Assuming no anger is being expressed, you should use one or more of the following methods to clarify the issues involved in the conflict.

Active Listening

Listening is hard work. A good listener is one who attends to what the other person is saying in such a way that he or she understands what that person is saying. The other person validates this understanding by means of statements like "Yeah," "Right," "Uh-huh," or by making eye contact with you. All these responses mean that the other person believes you understand what he or she is saying.

There are four skills essential to active listening: (1) reflecting content, (2) reflecting feeling, (3) paraphrasing, and (4) summarizing. An example of each follows. For further information, see *The Helping Relationship* by Lawrence Brammer (Englewood Cliffs, NJ: Prentice-Hall, 1973).

Reflecting Content

With this tactic you repeat back to the speaker his or her own words. When you mirror the speaker's statement in this way, he or she generally perceives you as displaying empathy or understanding. For more on this topic, see *Helping and Human Relations* by Robert Carkhuff (New York: Holt, Rinehart & Winston, 1969).

Here is an example from the case of Michael. The interaction that follows is from a phone conversation.

Principal: Please, Mrs. James, explain to me what is going on here.

Mrs. James: Well, I thought we could work it out with the counselor, but clearly this teacher [the English teacher] has to go. I will not have my son [Michael] in that class.

Principal: I hear you saying that you thought you could work it out, but at this point you want to change your son's English teacher.

Mrs. James: Yes, that is right.

Reflecting Feelings

This skill is similar to reflecting content. Now, however, you reflect the *feeling* associated with the speaker's verbal content. This is more demanding than reflecting content because it requires that you listen for the feeling words used in the conversation. Here is an example:

Mrs. James: I am annoyed that this so-called teacher would even attempt to meet with me.

Principal: You are annoyed about this teacher.

Mrs. James: Damn right I am! Furthermore, I am angry at the school district for allowing this character to even teach in this building.

Principal: You are annoyed and angry at the whole situation.

Mrs. James: I said I was and I am.

Notice that at the end of the exchange, Mrs. James acknowledges the principal's active listening by telling him that what he heard was what she was feeling—that he heard her correctly.

If the speaker uses no feeling words, you cannot easily reflect back feeling expressed. You may need to guess at the speaker's feeling. Your guess will often be accurate because the person's feelings are so dominant that they are ready to burst forth. Here is an example:

Mrs. James: Can you believe what he said to me? He had some nerve!

Principal: You were shocked that a teacher could say such a thing.

Mrs. James: Shocked is right.

Do not be afraid of making a wrong guess. Generally, the speaker will correct you and, in the process, reveal his or her true feelings.

Mrs. James: He said things to me I could not believe an adult would say to anyone.

Principal: You were shocked.

Mrs. James: Not shocked, I was mortified!

Paraphasing

This third skill involves making a concise response to the speaker. It is not simply repeating content or feeling but, rather, editing the speaker's words to get at the core of the message. A good paraphrase is concise, avoids the details, and uses the speaker's own words, as follows:

Mrs. James: I need to meet with you about this teacher. Perhaps I need to meet with the superintendent of schools. Who knows what should be done? But I will demand that something happen. Maybe he needs to be fired. Maybe I will have my friends picket his class. Maybe I will send a letter to the editor.

Principal: You want something to happen as a result of our meeting.

Summarizing

This last skill is useful if the conversation has lasted a long time or if you are meeting for a second or third time with the other person and want to remind him or her what was discussed before. A good summary is an integration of the content and the feelings that have been expressed. It skips over the specific examples used and ignores any side issues that may have arisen. It can be a powerful statement to someone who, after rambling on at length, has the issues reduced to a few key points. In the example here, the principal summarizes what Mrs. James has said:

Principal: If I can summarize what we have been saying here, Mrs. James, it seems to me that you are annoyed with this teacher, shocked at what he said to you, and that you want something to happen, but at this time you are not quite sure what it should be.

As important as active listening can be to convey a sense that you understand what the other person is saying, sometimes it is not a good idea to use it. This is true when:

- You feel the need to make a judgment call about what the other person is saying.
- You do not have the time to listen to it all.
- You do not trust the other person.

In summary, active listening means being attentive to another person in such a way that you can figuratively step into his or her shoes with regard to the issue. It is based on the belief that other people have a right to think and feel as they do, that they are ultimately the best source of change, and that all of us are individuals who need to be understood by others. Activity 3-1 will help you perfect your active listening skills.

ACTIVITY 3-1

The following are a number of remarks made by individuals. To understand the skills of active listening, compare your responses to each of these remarks to the responses at the end of the worksheet.

1. *Reflect content.* "I am very angry at the way the principal set this meeting up. He could have informed us of the problem."

   Response: _____

   _____

2. *Reflect feeling.* "There are two ways you could have done this project, the way you did it and the correct way. If you think I going to follow this book, you had better think twice."

   Response: _____

   _____

3. *Paraphrase.* "I am trying to set up the criteria for this alternative program, but I've had no success. The counselors will not have time to meet with me. Yet I know these counselors will be referring students to me. They do not even know what kind of student I work with. Now they want to add students to the program."

   Response: _____

   _____

4. *Summarize.* "I think we need a new office for the teacher center equipment. It would be an honor to have it in our building, and if we do not get such an office we will lose this golden opportunity. Maybe we need a building-level vote on whether we should give up one of the conference rooms for this."

   Response: _____

   _____

An active listener's responses to these remarks might be as follows:

1. You are angry at the way the principal set this meeting up.

2. You are angry that you are being asked to follow this book.

3. The criteria for the alternative program need to be clarified.

4. The teacher center offers an opportunity that requires a building-level vote.

Language

What we say and how we say it are important in every negotiation. The first concerns the content, the second the message. All participants in a settlement meeting hope to communicate their needs, positions, and demands to the other party in a clear, concise, and powerful manner that will influence the other. But most people wrongly assume that their own message is very clear (as it is to themselves) and that it is the listener who has failed in not understanding the message.

The meaning of a message is not in the speaker's intentions but, rather, in the listener's response. This statement deserves some thought because it goes against what most of us see as the purpose of language. In any interaction, all conversation has some behavioral value. Every statement, including silence, influences others. It is impossible, therefore, *not* to communicate with others. As people send and receive messages, patterns of interaction develop. People interpret messages on the basis of their own ideas. Their response to the original message prompts another message, which in turn causes a certain response.

This characteristic of language is seen in some examples of how language can be used to influence participants to clarify their interests.

Pace

When you communicate with another person, you use an unconscious pacing mechanism. This sensor allows you to make your verbal and nonverbal messages match the other person's readiness level, special needs, and personal history.

On the verbal level, pacing is seen in your choice of verbs. Although all people (assuming there are no physical handicaps) receive input through the five senses—visual, auditory, kinesthetic, tactile, and olfactory—under stress people tend to choose one of these modalities as the primary receiver of sensory input—that is, to favor one sense over another. To gain a clue to which sensory system is predominant, listen to the type of verbs used in the following examples:

A visual process: "I had to look your proposal over twice before I understood it."
An auditory process: "Say that to me again."

A kinesthetic process: "You know, I felt good about that idea of
    yours."
An olfactory process: "Something smells rotten with this deal."

For further reading in these areas see *Practical Magic* by Steve
Lankton (Cupertino, CA: Meta Publications, 1980).

In pacing, you try to match the modality system of the other
speaker in hopes of influencing the other by using a sensory input
system to which the other person can readily relate. For example,
you might respond to each of the foregoing statements by matching
the sensory modality, as follows:

Visual: "Yes, looking at it twice made it clearer to me."
Auditory: "Sure, let's discuss this issue again."
Kinesthetic: "Good. It does have a nice feeling to it."
Olfactory: "This is a foul-smelling deal."

Some other common words associated with the different sensory systems are listed here:

Visual: see, vision, picture, bright, peak, show, cloudy, perspec-
    tive, horizon
Auditory: discuss, hear, yell, noisy, told, listen, loud, shout
Kinesthetic: feel, irritated, frustrated, depressed, excited, ten-
    sion, energized
Olfactory: This modality is uncommon; however, words like *smell*
    and *sniff* are sometimes used.

In addition to verbal communication, you can also learn to
pace your nonverbal communication. Commonly, an administrator
will rise to talk to someone who has just entered his or her office.
This is a way of matching the other person's nonverbal pace. Mir-
roring the way the other speaker uses his or her body is another
way of matching. People can often be seen talking to each other
each with arms folded in the same way. If one person yawns, others
nearby are apt to repeat the behavior. These are examples of unconscious nonverbal pacing. Activity 3-2 will give you practice in
pacing.

Congruence

For a message to be received properly and forcefully, there must be
congruence between what is said and what is done. For example, if

---

ACTIVITY 3-2

The following are statements from various school personnel. Respond to each by trying to match the pace of the primary sensory system in use. Some typical responses are at the bottom of the worksheet.

Teacher: I can see the superintendent going crazy over this one.

Response: _____

_____

Principal: Let's all hear it for Mrs. Smith. She did a fine job on that assembly.

Response: _____

_____

Superintendent: I want all of you to get behind the budget vote. It is important to all of us. Let's get going and get out the vote.

Response: _____

_____

Board member: I don't want to complain, but this item in the budget is overinflated. I do not feel comfortable going to the public with this one.

Response: _____

_____

Typical responses are as follows:

1. *To the teacher:* He will probably see red. (*visual*)

2. *To the principal:* Yes, I told everyone to expect a surprise. (*auditory*)

3. *To the superintendent:* We will be going after it with every resource at our disposal. (*kinesthetic*)

4. *To the board member:* I wish you would feel more positive about this item. It affects every kid in the school. (*kinesthetic*)

you are listening to a student describing how he or she feels harassed in a school, you should not at the same time be looking out for a certain teacher to come through the door. At least at the unconscious level, and probably even at the conscious level, the student will become aware of the incongruence between what you are saying and what you are doing. To transmit the message that you understand, you need to focus your nonverbal behavior, in this case eye contact, onto the student.

EXAMPLE

This story, which may be apocryphal, comes out of the time in the 1960s when Albert Shanker, representing New York's United Federation of Teachers, was negotiating the New York City teachers' contract. The two sides, the union and the city council, sat down at the bargaining table to negotiate. Late in the morning, the city council representatives decided to stop the discussion for a while and send out for coffee and doughnuts. A secretary was called in and went around taking orders from each of the city council representatives. The city council did not ask the union representatives if they wanted anything to eat. The negotiators then took a short break while the coffee was brought in. Then, when the city council announced that everyone had had a coffee break and they were ready to negotiate, Shanker announced that he was now going to take a coffee order for his side of the table. The city council objected to the waste of time, but Shanker and his representatives left the room to get their coffee, leaving the city council members alone in the room.

This story illustrates what happens when two parties tell each other and the public that they will negotiate in good faith, but one of the parties then acts as though the other did not exist. By matching the behavior of the other party, Shanker brought to the city council's attention the incongruence of their action—and he did it without a word of direct explanation.

Another area of incongruence can develop when one party is influenced primarily by one sensory system and the other party is operating primarily from another system. An example of this is shown in the following exchange:

Elizabeth: I said that I wanted to hear from the teachers each Friday. I haven't heard a thing.

Assistant principal: I saw the teachers involved and they agreed to communicate with you. You should be getting something in the mail on this.

In summary, language is not only a process of communicating but also a means of establishing a positive relationship with others. By using the procedures described here, you can influence others and help clarify the interests of all the participants.

Information Seeking

To foster a more mutual understanding of what another party means by what he or she is saying, there is a series of questions you can ask. These questions elicit further information from the other person and help clarify the original statement. As the person's statements become clearer, it is assumed that his or her interests will become clearer as well.

Behind this series of questions is the belief that we all have a limited view of reality, confined to the small part we are able to perceive. We make generalizations about reality on the basis of this limited experience. The language we use reflects this limitation. By soliciting more information from a person, we can prompt that person to explore aspects of reality of which he or she may have been unaware. In time, that person's sense of reality expands and becomes broader. For our purposes, however, the point of this process is to elicit clarifying information about the issues involved.

Listed here are five common types of limitations that individuals impose on their reality. After each is an example of how to use questions to draw out further information. This information is adapted and used by permission of the author and publisher from Richard Bandler and John Grinder, *The Structure of Magic, I,* 1975. Copyright © 1975 Science and Behavior Books, Palo Alto, California.

Generalizations

People may make statements that are so inclusive that they limit any other view of a situation. These people usually take one situation or a few situations and generalize from them to encompass their entire sense of reality.

Jeannette: The problem with teachers is that they only think of
    what the school can do for them. They never think of others.
Rick: Is that a problem with *all* of the teachers in this building?
Jeannette: Well, not all. Maybe most.
Rick: And is it a problem that they *never* think of others?

Here Rick, the teacher, is trying to expand Jeannette's view of
teachers. He is challenging her limited view that all the teachers in
the building never think of anyone but themselves. Once he asks
her for information on her position, he is able to change her view
on the issue.

Deletions

People often delete information from their statements. They may
assume others know what is contained in the deleted parts. It is
wise to challenge these deletions because your questions can elicit
useful information.

Tom: I need more supplies. How can you expect me to teach without
    adequate supplies?
Evelyn: What supplies? Which ones are you referring to?
Tom: You know. I need more markers and stuff.
Evelyn: What stuff? You mentioned markers. Are there other spe-
    cific items you would like?

Here Evelyn is asking Tom to add to his statement that he needs
supplies. Tom has deleted so much from his statement that Evelyn
is not sure what he means. There is some doubt that Tom even
knows himself. By asking the question in this form, Evelyn forces
Tom to fill in the missing information.

Mind Reading

Another common error is trying to mind-read or guess what another person is thinking or feeling. It is true that if you are with
people over a period of time, you will be somewhat able to predict
what they might do. But you can be on thin ice if you try to read
someone's mind. Often we project our feelings onto others and call
our own feelings their feelings. Here are two examples of attempted
mind reading.

Bill: You know, school librarians don't like to let books leave the library. They don't feel in control unless all the books are on the shelves.

Anne: That principal feels that physical education teachers are second-class teachers, that they do not teach at all.

The quickest way to challenge such assumptions is to ask how the person arrived at that conclusion. There should be some experience that supports people's conclusions, and this information needs to be solicited to clarify the issue at hand. This is how to question the foregoing statements:

Principal: How does the librarian act in your school?

Principal: What has your principal said about physical education teachers?

Nominalizations

Words that are used as nouns in a sentence when they actually reflect an activity or process are called *nominalizations.* By using such words to present an active state as a static state, some people give the impression that everything is fixed and nothing can be changed. If these speakers use verbs to describe the state they refer to, they can make the process come alive, present the information more precisely, and reveal the issue more clearly. Following is an example of how a superintendent challenged the nominalizations of one of his principals.

Principal: Parents do not respect us. They always complain.

Superintendent: Who is not respecting you?

Principal: Those parents of the gifted children.

Superintendent: Which parent? Is there one or a few?

Principal: You know Mrs. Smith, don't you? She complains most of the time.

Superintendent: Well, what does she say that makes you feel that she is complaining?

First, the superintendent challenges the principal's generalization that *all* parents have no respect for him. Then the superintendent challenges the principal's static view of the term *respect.* Finally, he asks questions whose answers will turn the word *re-*

spect into a process or series of behaviors that Mrs. Smith is performing. The information gained here is helpful to the superintendent as he begins to clarify the conflict this principal is having with parents.

Confiners

Words that limit what people can do or say are referred to as *confiners*. Words like *must, cannot, always,* and *never* are examples; they confine the action of a person. In trying to focus on the specifics of a conflict issue, it is helpful to remove any terms that prevent such movement in the settlement phase. Following are a few statements containing confining words and examples of how to challenge them.

Lynn: I can't talk to that person.
Principal: What stops you?

Ginny: I must have a concession on this point.
Principal: And if it is not forthcoming?

   Activity 3-3 gives you an opportunity to test your information-seeking skills by providing responses to a number of statements.

Reframe

Reframing is just like what you would do if you took an old painting that you had been looking at for years and literally put a new frame on it. Suddenly, you would see the painting as new. Although the painting itself is the same, the background has changed.

   Reframing is an excellent tool to use with others to provide new clarity on an old problem. What has been perceived as a conflict is transformed into an asset. What seems to be, shifts and becomes something else. For example, a teacher who complains that she never sees her principal visiting her classroom may be persuaded that in fact the reason the principal never visits is that he trusts her to provide high-quality education.

   To work, reframing must be a valid process, not a con job on the other person but, rather, an honest attempt to portray an event in a different, more positive light. The reframe must be in the realm of possibility. Remember, the goal of the reframe is to provide the other person with a clearer view of the issue. What is first seen as a

———— ACTIVITY 3-3 ————

The statements listed here require a response. Use the different types of information-seeking skills you have just learned to direct the flow of this information. Answer each statement with a question that will provide you with more information about the specific thoughts of the speaker. Effective responses appear at the end of this worksheet. Compare your responses to these. In your opinion, which response would elicit more information from the speaker?

1. All administrators are seeking to move up in the field. They will not be in this building long. They use us.

    Response: _____

    _____

2. I need more support on this. Can you back me up?

    Response: _____

    _____

3. The people in this district are indifferent to what clubs are run.

    Response: _____

    _____

4. The students of today are different. They lack motivation to succeed. They are problem students. Education needs to do something.

    Response: _____

    _____

5. I can't keep being the one who gets the summer school in my building.

    Response: _____

    _____

Some typical responses are as follows:

1. Does every administrator act like this? Do I? (*generalization*)

2. What do you mean by *support?* What do you see me doing specifically? (*deletion*)

3. How do you know they are indifferent? Can you mind-read? (*mind reading*)

4. What is *motivation?* What do you mean by this? (*nominalization*)

5. And if you get it next year, what are you going to do? (*confiner*)

problem and a source of conflict may in fact be something entirely different.

Two examples to illustrate reframing follow.

EXAMPLES

The movie *Patton* contains a scene in which Patton is being flown over the English Channel to be given a new assignment. The time is after D-Day, a critical period in the Allies' attempt to retake France. On the flight over, Patton is angrily complaining to everyone on the plane about having to ride a cargo plane to get to the war. He feels that something more elegant would show more respect for his status. One of his more astute aides listens for awhile and then suggests that Patton has been assigned to the cargo plane because this plane is loaded with high-priority equipment that is urgently needed to ensure victory. Patton likes this interpretation, or reframing, of the cargo plane assignment. It fits his view of his own importance and puts an end to his complaints.

A second example is the story of an elementary school principal who went to the middle school one day and found herself walking through the cafeteria at lunchtime. Many students called out her last name, and soon others started chanting her name. Some students pounded the tables. The principal was embarrassed. She waved, but she felt teased and abused by these students. She mentioned the incident to the middle school principal and told him how she felt. It seemed to her that the students disliked her.

The middle school principal started to laugh and said he felt amused by the whole incident. Caught off guard, his colleague asked how he could laugh at such a thing. He reminded her that often middle school students do not know how to express their emotions properly. They just act the way they feel. He asked her, "Did you expect them to applaud? Or would you have preferred it if they ignored you?" The elementary principal said no to both questions. Then the middle school principal reframed the event and explained the chanting and pounding as expressions of the students' positive response to his colleague. They were glad to see her! After considering this for a minute, she said that he was right. The students had responded appropriately for the situation, and in fact she now felt flattered by their attention.

To engage in reframing, you need to listen carefully to what the other person is saying and consider other possible interpretations of the event. Coming up with these interpretations may mean listening to your own feelings about the event. How you feel about it may give you a clue to a new way to frame it. Once you have a new frame to try out, interrupt the other person abruptly to shift the tone of the pattern that person is developing. Say something like "Wow!" or "Really?" or "That's fantastic!" or use nonverbal gestures such as smiling, laughing, standing up, or shaking hands. These are all examples of pattern interrupters. Then explain the new frame you would like the other person to consider. Allow enough time for the frame to sink in and for the other person to make it fit properly. Do not expect a quick response. The new frame may take a long time to fit into the other person's cognitive perception. When and if it does fit, the other person will most likely affirm it for you. In any case, you can be assured that the person will think about it even if he or she initially rejects it outright.

Metaphor

This is probably the most evident skill used in conflict resolution meetings. Because the atmosphere in these meetings can be so highly charged, with major policy decisions hanging on the words of the participants, the people involved may revert to using an indirect way of communicating. Although the message is delivered with a powerful force, it is less risky than a direct statement. Most of the sending and receiving of messages is done at an unconscious level. The real pros in negotiating constantly use metaphors with a great deal of sophistication.

What is a metaphor? It is the use of a story to deliver a message by expressing one thing in terms of another. The plot and characters in the story represent the situation and the individuals in the conflict resolution meeting. But this representation is so far removed from the real situation that the resemblance can be hard to figure out. The metaphor organizes the experience in a way that clarifies the issues for all involved.

As an illustration, recall the story of Albert Shanker at his teachers' union bargaining meeting with representatives of New York City (see the earlier section on congruence). Whether or not the story is literally true does not matter. Some negotiators use this story at the beginning of a session. Usually everyone laughs at the notion of these representatives feuding over coffee and doughnuts.

Yet at the same time a message is delivered to everyone of the participants in the room. That message is designed to assure everyone that all participants are bargaining in good faith and that there is room in the settlement for all sides to gain jointly.

Other metaphors can be jokes or one-liners. At the beginning of one bargaining session, an off-color joke was told in mixed company. Although the women were offended, there was a lot of laughter. The message delivered indirectly at the start of this meeting was that women would have a lower status than men in the negotiating process.

There are two ways to enhance a metaphor. One way is to embed something into the story line to make your point. The easiest and most common way to do this is to use someone's name. For example, you might say, "So there's this skunk. Frank, you know how a skunk smells. Well, this skunk gets into the building and starts to . . ." The embedded item here, the name "Frank," associates Frank directly with the skunk analogy. If Frank does not get the message that he is disliked through the story, the embedded use of his name certainly drives home the association.

A second way to enhance the metaphor is to raise or lower your voice when you speak as a way of emphasizing a particular part of the story. For example, you might say: "There was this rose in the garden; *it was so peaceful to look at.* Anyway, this rose was a reminder to everyone that beauty could be found even among the thorns. *It was so peaceful to look at. . . .*" The italics in this excerpt show where the storyteller lowered her voice to put an emphasis on the peaceful environment that the rose established. In this case, the speaker was trying to transfer this peaceful ethos to the negotiation process.

To be successful, a metaphor needs to be built following these steps:

1. Examine the problem.
2. Identify the primary individuals involved in the problem and match them with characters, animals, or objects in a story.
3. Select a story line that matches the narrative of the problem.
4. Provide a desired solution to the story line.

In using metaphors, remember that they are present at most conflict resolution meetings, that they are usually unconscious, and that they present clear information about the intentions of the initiator.

Questioning

The last skill to use to clarify the issue is probably also the easiest—questioning. You can ask a direct or indirect question of the other participant in order to elicit information about the issue. This skill is particularly helpful in developing objective data to support the interests of the two participants. It is much easier to discuss an issue if there are some hard facts to back up each of the opposing interests.

Direct Questioning

The purpose of direct questioning is to elicit a lot of information about the issue from the other participant. Although you do gain information quickly in this way, there is a drawback. The other participant often will ramble on in giving the answer. Therefore, direct questioning needs to be structured. The following are a number of questions that can provide you with information about the issue:

- What is the problem here?
- What happened to bring you to this situation?
- What do you think needs to be done?
- What are the common issues here?
- Do you want to explore these issues?
- Are you looking for a quick answer?
- Do you have time to look at a number of possible solutions?
- Are there others who should be present or involved?
- Is there some evidence to support your claim?
- Where can we get information to back you up?

Indirect Questioning

This type of questioning seeks no specific answer. It is vague enough to elicit a broad spectrum of information about a situation. Here are a few examples of this type of questioning:

- When will you know you have resolved this problem?
- When will you feel (or hear, or see) you have resolved this prob-

lem? (The verb in this question can be chosen to match the primary sensory modality system of the participant.)

- What would happen right now if I gave in to all of your demands?
- What would happen right now if you gave in to all of my demands?
- What would happen if we both dropped a single demand?
- What would happen if we delayed this resolution meeting for two days? For a week? A month? Two months?
- Can you elaborate on that answer?
- Can you give me an example of what you mean?
- If the facts were different, would your interest here be different?

Questioning was listed last in this series of clarification skills because it is the one skill everyone uses at one time or other during a meeting. The fact that it is the most common, however, does not mean that it provides the clearest answers. The other skills described in this section should be used as well, as they provide a rich insight into the issues behind a problem.

MICHAEL'S CONFLICT

(Please read the section at the end of Chapter Two to find out what preceded this part of the conflict resolution meeting.)

Both Mr. and Mrs. James were present at the meeting, along with the guidance counselor and the principal. The English teacher was in the faculty room, and Michael was in class.

As everyone was getting settled, there was some small talk about the weather. Mrs. James told a metaphoric story that described exactly how she was feeling about this meeting and what she expected the outcome to be. The principal and the counselor were tense because of the previous threats and animosity that had been expressed. But once the story had been told, they were able to gain an insight into Mrs. James's interests. Here is the story:

Mrs. James: Spring must be here now. It has been a long winter, but what I saw from my bedroom window brought hope back into my old bones. I saw crocuses popping out from under the snow. They are beautiful in color. Winter was hard this year. Spring is here, I hope!

The principal began the meeting by summarizing why everyone was gathered in his office:

Principal: We are meeting here to discuss the issue of Michael's English grade as well as his placement in Mr. Fritz's class. Mrs. James has requested this meeting.

Mrs. James: Yes, thank you. As I have said before, I think Mr. Fritz is out to get my son. He gave him an F, and I do not see it as appropriate. I asked for but did not see any evidence that Michael deserves an F. I want his grade changed to at least a B, and I want him out of that man's class.

Here Mrs. James stated her positions in the form of two demands. She expressed a primary visual modality ("see it," "see any evidence").

Mr. James: Yes, that is right. We have a record of all that Michael has done in the class. We asked him to give us a list of assignments he did not complete for the teacher. Here they are. According to our records, Michael has completed all but one assignment. Does that mean he gets an F? Come on, now. Where's the fairness in that?

Here Mr. James revealed his primary sensory system, which was similar to that of his wife. This congruence in their thinking provided an easy sensory match for the principal to use to gain a clear picture of the conflict.

Principal: As I see your demands here, there are two: first, that Michael be given a grade that is equal to the work he has done, and second, that Michael be removed to another class. You have some records here to support these issues.

The principal here used an active listening skill (reflecting content) to demonstrate that he understood the parents' viewpoint. Notice that he avoided the use of a reflecting feeling statement because there was some doubt in his mind about the parents' congruence with regard to feelings. On the phone prior to the meeting Mrs. James expressed angry feelings; yet her metaphor contained feelings of hope and clarity. It was not the principal's purpose here to clarify the parents' feelings, as they themselves probably were not sure of their feelings. The principal was willing to let the feelings remain ambiguous for the time being and focus instead on what people were saying. He decided to state his interest in the matter and to allow the counselor to do so as well.

Principal: Well, my position here is twofold. First, I must preserve the grading process at the school. I cannot unilaterally change grades that teachers have given. Second, I am concerned about whether Michael is really learning the course. Does he, in fact, know and understand the subject matter? It doesn't matter what grade he receives if he does not understand the material.

Counselor: Yes, I agree. I want everyone involved, especially Michael, to feel comfortable with the settlement. After all, it is Michael's interests that are at stake here.

The principal here stated his interests, not his positions. He told the parents that he had no preconceived settlement in mind but would consider any options as long as his interests were satisfied. He shifted the focus away from Michael's grade onto the issue of knowledge. In doing so, he hoped to model to the parents a process of moving from a static position (Michael's specific grade) to a flexible interest (Michael's understanding of the subject matter).

The counselor also expressed an interest rather than a position. She did this using a kinesthetic sensory modality ("feel comfortable"). If you did some further investigation, you would expect her to have a behaviorist administrative style. (See Chapter Seven for a description of the various administrative styles.)

Mrs. James: Of course we are interested in Michael. He is our primary concern. And we do not want to mess with the school's grading system. However, there is no way of knowing what he has learned from this man. Who knows? At least his report card can look good, and at least you can change the class assignment. I have here a record of his assignments, and there is only one he did not complete.

Mrs. James acknowledged that she had heard the principal and the counselor's statements. Yet she reverted to her position statement and used the record sheet of assignments as a focal point. The principal decided to use this record and draw from it further information that might open up the interests under discussion.

Principal: Mrs. James, perhaps I can use this record sheet of assignments that you have to determine what Michael has learned in this course. I am going next door to see Mr. Fritz and ask him to tell me what grade he gave Michael on each of these assignments. We need his input here.

According to plan, the principal was keeping Mr. Fritz separate from the meeting. He now acted as a mediator between the parents and the teacher without the two ever seeing each other. The following is a description of the events that occurred as the principal went back and forth between the two rooms to share information.

When he saw the teacher, the principal discovered that Michael was doing D work on the assignments. He also discovered that Michael owed the teacher three more assignments. That was why the teacher had failed Michael. The parents' response was that Michael had completed two of the missing three assignments but felt it was fruitless to turn them in because the teacher hated him. The parents claimed that Michael had these two assignments in his locker now.

When he heard that Michael had completed two assignments, the teacher told the principal he would concede on the F and regrade these two missing assignments. The parents refused to consider this option because they felt the teacher would grade both papers as F's and Michael would still have an F on his report card. They simply did not trust the teacher. When the teacher heard this position, he told the principal that he wanted Michael out of his class because now he could not trust Michael. He wanted the F to stand.

At this point in the conflict, the teacher and the parents locked horns. The teacher gave up trying to keep Michael in the class. This was a minor concession, but one that would turn out to be of value, as we shall see in the next chapter.

Activity 3-4 gives you a chance to outline your actions in a recent conflict, in order to see how you were able to disengage from demands.

TACTIC 2: DISENGAGING FROM ANGER

Often there is a need to disengage the participants in a conflict from their opening remarks. As we discussed earlier, these opening remarks usually involve stating a position. At times, however, one or more of the participants in a conflict come to a negotiation full of anger. Usually, there is a long history of hurt associated with conflicts. When the time comes to reach a settlement, it is only natural for these hurts to surface and express themselves in angry

ACTIVITY 3-4

As you enter into a conflict resolution meeting, it is wise to keep notes on important events. Recall a conflict you had in the past week and try to complete the responses to the questions described below. Outlining the information may help you understand how you disengaged from demands.

Write the demands that were made:

1. _____

2. _____

3. _____

4. _____

List the primary sensory system present. Explain why you think it is present.

Visual_____

Auditory_____

Kinesthetic_____

Olfactory_____

Write any statements you feel were reframed. How were they reframed, in your opinion?

_____

_____

_____

Were there metaphors present? If yes, write here how the speaker used each metaphor and how it met the criteria listed in the text.

_____

_____

_____

_____

Was there other information presented that you feel is pertinent? If so, explain why you feel this information is important to remember later in negotiations.

_____

_____

_____

_____

_____

demonstrations. You cannot negotiate successfully when intense anger is present. You need to handle the anger before clarification of issues can begin. There are a number of strategies that you can use to help the different participants deal with demonstrations of anger at conflict resolution meetings.

Before these strategies are presented, however, you are asked to test your skill at handling anger. Activity 3-5 will give you an idea how you respond to anger.

Strategies for Responding to Anger

Ignore It

Sometimes you can ignore anger directed at you. In our case of Michael, the parents were angry with the English teacher and had expressed this anger to the principal many times. At the actual meeting, however, the principal decided to ignore any feelings of anger expressed by the parents. His primary reason was that he felt the parents were ambiguous about their feelings. Rather than deal with their anger, he decided to let it slip in the hope that once the parties got involved in the actual negotiation process, their anger would be a side issue.

Sometimes a negotiation meeting begins with a blast of anger from one or both sides. That blast is usually all there is to the anger. Once it is expressed, it is over with. The trick is not to react to the outburst but to let it slip by. If you try to deal with it, the other party will become fixated on it, and no one will be able to get past it. This is especially true if an angry outburst from one party leads to a reciprocal angry outburst from the other. The opening outburst is often used as part of one participant's bargaining strategy as a way of showing how much that party means business. Here is an example of how an angry outburst can be ignored:

ACTIVITY 3-5

This activity tests your skill at handling anger. Read the following statements and fill in your response on the lines provided.

1. I am tired of your indifference to my situation. Let's get with it!

   Response: _____

   _____

2. The problem with administrators is that they do not know how to teach.

   Response: _____

   _____

3. The switching of classes was a mess. I ended up with 30 students. You really blew it this time.

   Response: _____

   _____

4. I am tired of her laziness. Why don't you confront her on this? You are the administrator. Do something!

   Response: _____

   _____

   _____

   In reviewing your responses, look to see if any pattern of response has developed. Have you tried to deny the other person's anger by not responding to it? Perhaps you tried to argue back, or tried to blame the situation on someone else. All of these responses would be legitimate. There is no right or wrong method for dealing with anger. Often, nothing works. The anger just needs to run its course. With some practice, however, you may find that the procedures to be described here, used singly or together, may defuse potentially destructive meetings. For further reading, see *Special Educators' Discipline Handbook* by R. Maurer (West Nyack, NY: The Center for Applied Research in Education, 1988).

Katie: That was one of the dumbest things I ever saw. What made you think you could get away with it? I'm furious!

Joseph: I understand that you're angry. Perhaps we could move on with the matter at hand.

Katie: I just wish you had consulted with me about this. You really know how to keep me mad.

Joseph: As I said, there are a lot of issues to deal with here. We need to discuss them.

Notice how Joseph acknowledged the anger but ignored Katie's need to talk about it. Instead, he kept bringing her back to the task at hand. If someone rambles on in anger, you can use the same skill by continually bringing up a focal point so that, when the rambling has run its course, the person has somewhere else in the conversation to go. Here are two examples:

Joseph: Katie, can we come back to the point here?

or

Joseph: Katie, I said I understand your point. Can we move on? We need to focus on Agenda I.

Agree with It

This skill will actually defuse the situation. It usually works, but it requires that you keep your ego away from the problem. Here you acknowledge that the reason for the anger may be true. There is no discussion of the anger, just a statement to support its validity. The result will be an immediate reduction in the intensity of the anger. Here is how Joseph could have responded to Katie's statement:

Joseph: Well, at the time it seemed like the right thing to do. Now, perhaps I have second thoughts.

or

Joseph: Well, I regret that what I did made you angry.

Redirect It

This is a common method of dealing with anger. Rather than ignoring it or agreeing with it, you tell the person that he or she is angry at the wrong source. The real problem lies somewhere else. The trouble with this approach is that it can make a scapegoat out of another person. You certainly do not want to direct someone to be angry at another person if there are no grounds to support it. However, you do need to be honest with the other person and give the facts as you see them. (Often, what you consider the facts are in re-

ality your own analysis of the data.) If, in your opinion, the reason
the person is angry has to do with another source, you need to tell
that person why. Here is an example:

Ginny: Joseph, you're a bum! You told the principal that I left early
      on Tuesday, and now he's all over my case. Thanks for
      nothing!

Joseph: Now, wait a minute. I didn't tell him directly. There was a
      phone call for you, and he came looking for you in your room. I
      told him you had left. What was I going to do—have him look
      all over the building for you? He was doing you a favor trying to
      hook you up with the phone call. Don't worry, he gets like
      that. It won't amount to anything.

Ginny: Oh, I'm sorry. I didn't know all the facts on this. I didn't
      mean to jump all over you.

Another common dynamic of anger is that it can be displaced
onto one or more of the negotiators during an intense negotiation
process. It is hard to get angry at a process. As a result, one of the
participants may hook his or her frustration onto a word or gesture
from one of the opposing participants. In cases like this it is a good
idea to redirect the anger back to the source—the process.

Principal: I'm tired of this. Why don't you go after that teacher?
      Fire the bum. Why do we have to dance around here and make
      a schedule that fits his teaching weaknesses? You are too
      passive.

Superintendent: Yes, we do have to play games for the sake of the
      peace and harmony of all involved. Working on this schedule
      can be frustrating. Remember, I was not the one who origi-
      nated the contract behind it. If you're angry, get angry at the
      contract, or, better yet, get involved in the next round of nego-
      tiations and try to get some of it altered.

Make It Absurd

This is a radical departure from the other skills described. Rather
than trying to minimize the anger or deal with it quickly and move
on, this skill requires the individual to stick with the anger and

even to escalate it. The procedure involves seizing the anger the other person is expressing and drawing it out to the point of absurdity. In the process, you point out to the other person how ridiculous the anger can be. This allows both parties to move on in the negotiation process.

This procedure is easy to use and, with humor, moves quickly. It requires that you accept the other person's anger and add to it. Then the other person responds to your addition, you respond again by adding, the other person tries to get out of the escalation, you add again, and finally the thought pattern is broken and the anger and all the additions collapse. Here is an example:

Teacher's union representative: The teachers have demanded that we have a choice in the class period that we teach at the high school. Some like to come in early and others like to come in late. This issue is a major one, and we will not move on any other issue unless we have a choice of flexible starting times. I am sure there are enough people who want to start early and others who want to start late to make this work. But understand: This is a demand.

Superintendent: I do understand. You know, I agree with you. In fact, it's such a good idea that I'm sure we can make it work for everyone. You will, of course, help us to implement it.

Teachers' union representative: Of course. It won't work without our involvement.

Superintendent: Good. Now I think we need to get all the teachers together and have them work out a master schedule that accommodates everyone. You could use the auditorium. I will ask the district media people to provide you with large overhead projectors and plenty of large writing tablets. Let's see, I would guess three or four meetings should do it. Which days after school do you want to meet?

Teachers' union representative: We can't ask every teacher to be part of this. The crowd would be huge. We wouldn't get anything done.

Superintendent: Well, get a committee together to figure it out. Perhaps 20 to 30 people could do it. It's a matter of coordinating everyone's wishes. I guess the ad hoc committee you will chair should be able to handle the requests of the other 150 teachers.

Teachers' union representative: What? Can you imagine what a task that would be? We're not prepared to do this. It's your job.

Superintendent: Yes, but you said everyone would need to be involved to get this done.

Teachers' union representative: Well, not everyone. That meeting would result in chaos. We cannot have everyone involved. Nothing would happen. No one would be happy. By the end they would all be after me.

Superintendent: I'm confused. You said everyone had to be involved to get it done right.

Teachers' union representative: Forget it! Forget it!

Superintendent: O.K. Perhaps here we could talk about what the teachers' interests are with regard to the schedule. What are their needs? We have agreed that their position of flexible hours won't work here.

Walk Away

This may seem a drastic step, but in a relative sense it can be an effective skill. This is especially true if the anger turns into a vicious or humiliating personal attack. When the anger is out of control or you judge that the other party is incapable of disengaging, you need to walk away. Walking away signals to the other person that you will not trade personal attacks, nor will you continually accept blame. Your message is that you are willing to negotiate but you will not do so under such circumstances.

Walking away can take different forms. Some administrators will excuse themselves to go to the rest rooms or to get a cup of coffee and then come right back to the meeting. They do this in the hope that this brief interlude will be enough to break the focus of the attack. Other administrators will try to focus the conversation away from the anger and onto an agenda or document that is being distributed. Although no one leaves the room here, shifting the focus onto another object is a form of walking away. It is particularly effective if some significant activity occurs to redirect the focus—for example, if the administrator gets up and calls his secretary, who then walks around the room distributing an agenda or other document. The principal may then ask everyone present to take a minute to scan the document. The enforced silence that follows may be all that is needed to break the anger.

Then, of course, there is the option of walking away from the meeting and not coming back. Sometimes this is the only alternative. Do not do it unless you have developed your BATNA (best alternative to a negotiated agreement). As discussed in Chapter Two, a BATNA is your final option. It should truly be a gain that is better than being on the receiving end of a severe attack of anger. If analyzed properly, a BATNA can be very attractive in a meeting. The main thing to remember is that a BATNA is not a position statement but an interest to be gained.

Counterattack

Sometimes you need to confront anger head on, especially if it becomes a personal, vindictive attack. To do so, you must have courage, be confident in what you are about to say, and not let it get personal. If you make a personal attack on your attacker, you will only fan the flames. Attack on the basis of the facts. You need to do this in a logical, step-by-step procedure, devoid of emotional outbursts. At times this can be hard. Remember, the task is to disengage from anger, not add your own anger to it. Keeping to the facts means that the focus does not vary. Here is an example of how one assistant superintendent used this skill:

Principal: You always put me last. It's as if my school is the least important. Everyone is tired by the time they get to my agenda. No one cares. You don't care. It's about time my school got some recognition from you.

Assistant superintendent: I know you are angry. First off, not everyone is tired by the time you get to talk about your school. Second, I do give your school recognition. Don't you remember how I called you only yesterday to commend you on the fine job you did in front of the board? Third, the president of the board of education picked the order, not I. I think you are off base in your attack.

Activity 3-6 is an opportunity to review the various ways of handling anger.

ACTIVITY 3-6

There are many valid ways to handle anger. No single way will be appropriate every time. To demonstrate this, you should review the various methods of dealing with anger. In the next week, attempt to use one of the methods when you find yourself dealing with an angry person. Here, you are asked to reflect on what happened and analyze the results.

ANALYSIS

What is the situation in which this encounter took place?

_____

_____

Which method did you choose to deal with the anger? Why did you pick this one?

_____

_____

_____

What did you do?

_____

_____

What did the other person do?

_____

_____

_____

In your estimation, how did the other person feel after this encounter?

_____

_____

_____

How did you feel?

_____

If you could do it over again, would you choose the same method? Why or why not?

SUMMARY

In this section the following skills were discussed: active listening, language, information seeking, mind reading, reframing, metaphor, and questioning. The use of any of these skills will give you a wealth of information about the issues or interests involved in a conflict. Using a number of these skills together increases your power to elicit this information. The purpose of gaining information should be emphasized. The participants in the resolution process need to focus on their interests in the conflict, not on their respective initial positions. Use of the skills described here will keep participants' attention on their interests rather than on their demands. Remember, if you focus only on positions, your settlement will be in terms of a position. If you focus on interests, however, your settlement will be in terms of satisfying your real needs.

Sometimes the opening remarks in a negotiation are expressions of anger or even threats. Like position statements or demands, these demonstrations call for disengagement. The negotiator has the option of ignoring the anger, agreeing with it, redirecting it, making the anger seem absurd, or walking away from it. No negotiation can occur while one or more of the parties are involved in angry outbursts or threatening postures.

MICHAEL'S CONFLICT

In the case of Michael, the principal decided to ignore any possible angry outburst from the parents. On the phone they expressed a great deal of anger. Yet the metaphor Mrs. James used in her opening statement was not one of anger. Also, the principal had asked the teacher not to be present in order to minimize the potential for hostile outbursts.

SUGGESTED READINGS

Gladstein, Deborah, & Reilly, Nora P. (1985, September). "Group Decision Making under Threat: The Tycoon Game." *Academy of Management Journal, 28,* 613–627.

Gordon, David. (1978). *Therapeutic Metaphors.* Cupertino, CA: META Publications.

Iklé, Fred Charles. (1973). "Bargaining and Communication." In Ithiel de Sola Pool & Wilbur Schramm (Eds.), *Handbook of Communication* (pp. 168–175). Boston: Houghton Mifflin.

Lewicki, Roy, & Litterer, J. R. (1985). *Negotiation: Reading Exercises and Cases.* Homewood, IL: Richard D. Irwin.

Maidment, Robert. (1985). "Conflict: A Conversation about Managing Differences." (Pamphlet). Reston, VA: National Association of Secondary School Principals.

Marongui, Pietro, & Newman, Graeme. (1987). *Vengeance: The Fight against Injustice.* Totowa, NJ: Rowman and Littlefield.

Quinn, Robert E. (1988). *Beyond Rational Management: Mastering the Paradoxes and Competing Demands of High Performance.* San Francisco: Jossey-Bass.

Saraydar, Edward. (1984, September). "Modeling the Role of Conflict and Conciliation in Bargaining." *Journal of Conflict Resolution, 28,* 420–450.

Tedeschi, James T. (1970). "Threats and Promises." In Paul Swingle (Ed.), *The Structure of Conflict.* New York: Academic Press.

CONFLICT RESOLUTION GUIDE

Each chapter in this book contains a Conflict Resolution Guide. You can use this guide as a worksheet for any ongoing conflict resolutions in which you are involved. It can serve as a checklist for determining where you are in the resolution process and where you need to go.

1. At the beginning of the conflict resolution meeting, listen for the other party's verbalized position statements or demands. If there has been prior publicity, you may already be aware of these positions or demands. List the major ones here:

   _____

   _____

   _____

   _____

2. Choose a disengagement strategy:

   Active listening _____

   Language _____

   Information seeking _____

   Reframing _____

   Metaphor _____

   Questioning _____

3. If anger is expressed during the opening of the talks, you will first need to record the statement here and then choose a method to help the other party disengage from it.

   Anger _____

   Method:

   Ignore it _____

   Agree with it _____

   Redirect it _____

   Make it absurd _____

   Walk away _____

   Counterattack _____

CHAPTER FOUR

Resolving Conflict

It is now time to bring the bargaining talks to a successful conclusion. You have disengaged the other party from position statements and have dealt with any anger and hurt feelings that have been present. Now you need to keep the momentum moving forward.

This chapter will demonstrate two additional tactics for moving the conflict toward resolution. Tactic 3 demonstrates how to apply pressure on the participants to settle. This is often necessary. At times, it is feasible for a party to refuse to settle or to delay the settlement process for as long as possible. For various reasons, you may find yourself in the position of needing to exert some leverage on everyone to make a commitment to settle. Tactic 4 shows how to discover different ways to settle once the commitment to resolve the conflict has been made by the participants. You will need to learn a number of skills and procedures that will allow you to generate a list of possible settlement options. This ability to move the settlement in many possible directions gives you a significantly greater chance to settle the conflict successfully.

These two tactics—exerting pressure to settle and finding ways to settle—are at the core of the conflict resolution process.

TACTIC 3: APPLYING PRESSURE TO SETTLE

Using Threats to Pressure

One tactic you should avoid at all costs is the use of threats. A threat is made when one party states that some drastic action will occur if that side's positional demands are not met. This party is in fact making a commitment to action. Threats are often used at the beginning of negotiations as a bluffing tactic. Yet a threat has power only if it is public, believable, and irreversible. In other words, everyone involved must be aware of the threat, it cannot merely be implied, and it must be an action that you know the other party not only can carry out but can carry out effectively. Finally, the threat, once taken, must be of such a nature that there is no way for the events to be undone.

Trying to threaten another party into seeking a settlement or accepting your terms reduces the negotiation process to positional bargaining. This means that one party will win and the other will lose. This win–lose strategy for resolving conflicts, as discussed in Chapter One, only leads to more conflict over the long haul. There is no evidence that threats produce more concessions from the other party.

To understand this point, recall the famous air traffic controllers' strike of 1981. The air traffic controllers issued a public, credible, and irreversible threat that they would leave their jobs if their demands were not met. Their threat had power because no one believed that President Reagan would fire them all. But President Reagan was not willing to be forced into positional bargaining by a threat statement. He had a different BATNA: He fired thousands of air traffic controllers in a single day. Their threat only led to further conflict.

Extensive research on the use of threats as a bargaining tactic has confirmed that there is about a 33 percent chance of a threatening statement prompting the other party to reciprocate with a similar type of statement. See *Bargaining: Power, Tactics, and Outcomes* by Samuel B. Bacharach and Edward J. Lawler (San Francisco: Jossey-Bass, 1988, p. 151). If the threatening statement is strong and is perceived by the other party as a punishment for not reaching settlement, there is about a 50 percent chance that such a punishment will be reciprocated by a similar punishing action by the other party. This can be seen in the case of a school building staff who decide to put pressure on the superintendent of schools to settle a conflict by following the letter of the contract and doing only the minimum required. They feel that this will intensify the pressure, but the superintendent sees it as a tactic of punishment. He immediately reciprocates by canceling all future negotiation meetings. As a result, there is now a stand-off, with both parties locked into positional bargaining and neither side willing to lose face by backing down.

Citing the Advantages of Settling

If you find yourself in a position where there is a lack of movement, there are a number of strategies that may be helpful to you. They may be used individually or combined to produce the needed movement. Some of these strategies involve citing the advantages of settling. Others, to be discussed in the next section, are ways of intensifying the pressure to settle.

Citing Relationship

Negotiations between individuals who know or have had dealings with each other are built on the participants' mutual knowledge and understanding. This knowledge usually includes an internal appraisal of the other, memories of some distinctive actions or remarks, and some personal background information on the other person. You can lean on this relationship a bit in order to move the negotiations forward and keep a positive momentum going. Here is an example:

Sue: Now, Bob, we have known each other for years. You know I won't cheat you on this one. I know you won't cheat me on this one either. Can we find a mutually agreeable settlement here?

If the relationship is new but you know that the relationship is going to exist for a long while, you may draw on this aspect, as in this example:

Sue: Now, Bob, we don't know each other very well, but I suspect you and I will be talking about other matters in the near future. Don't you think it serves our best interests to move toward a settlement here?

Citing Cost

The cost of negotiating can be prohibitive, especially if outside lawyers or consultants are used. The largest costs in schools are usually hidden—teachers who have to miss teaching time, administ-
trators who are not in their buildings, superintendents who are not
attending to board matters. This becomes a misallocation of resources. For parents involved in disputes, the cost of time from
their job or business can be large. These costs are not usually considered but can be damaging. Often, citing the continued cost of
not moving toward settlement is enough to get things moving.

Citing Stress

The pressure of negotiating causes stress. It is unavoidable. Some
people enjoy the tension involved in making deals. For most people,
however, the stress associated with resolving conflicts is something they prefer to avoid. Reminding the other party of the additional stress that a prolonged conflict will create can be an
incentive to resolve the conflict. A few people will try to use stress
to force the other participant to concede a position. This type of
game playing is described in detail in Chapter Six. Here, the purpose is not to *cause* stress but, rather, to use its existence to move
the other party to settlement. Here is an example:

Stevie: There is little point in going over this issue again. I cannot
deal with the added tension this is causing in my building. I
know you are getting pressure from the superintendent to resolve the issue. Let's see if we can find a settlement soon.

Citing Time

Time is measured differently in a school building than it is in the
real world or in the central administration building. Most schools
run by the ring of bells marking the beginning or end of a class period. As any teacher knows, you can be in the midst of a heated discussion, but when the bell rings for the next class, everyone will
move. The discussion ends, usually with no conclusion, and whatever is said probably has no bearing on what the teacher faces in
the next class period. Because of these time constraints, many negotiation meetings in schools revolve around a 40- to 50-minute
time period. If the meetings are held after school, the staff, teachers, and administrators are usually tired. They may have more

time to meet, but their fatigue level is higher. Again, time is a deter-mining factor.

Administrators who occupy offices removed from a school building and the tyranny of the bells perceive time differently. Con-flict meetings can go on longer if necessary. People can meet when they are not tired. There is generally more time to clarify issues, disengage from angry demonstrations, and generate a settlement. Therefore, exerting leverage to settle by citing time constraints is done more easily at a school building level than at a central office level. You can use time to move people to settle when it is to every-one's advantage to move things along so that teachers can get to class, administrators can get to the lunchroom or to bus dismissal, or parents can get to work.

Citing Your BATNA

Having a well-thought-out BATNA, or best alternative to a negoti-ated agreement, can work to your advantage. First, it removes the mental pressure you may feel to reach a settlement. Second, it gives you a criterion for measuring any settlement offered. Reveal-ing your BATNA to the other party can be a way of exerting leverage to settle. The other party now knows you have an option not to set-tle that is attractive to you. This puts pressure on the other side to commit to reaching a settlement. Here is an example:

Anne: I would like very much to consider your service proposal in our settlement. However, to date you have not given me dates or times of implementation. We need to move toward settle-ment on this computer budget. Otherwise, I will be forced to consider this very attractive proposal from your competitor. I would not like to do that because it is unfair to you and I think your company has something to offer us in this field. But at the moment you give me no alternative. Can we resolve this?

Activity 4-1 gives you some practice at citing the advantages of settlement.

Intensifying the Pressure to Settle

There are several options you may use to increase the pressure to settle. These may be invoked if you have no luck using the five methods outlined in the previous section. These techniques are not

---

ACTIVITY 4-1

As an administrator responsible for coordinating the curriculum among the different grade levels and the different school buildings in your district, you have worked closely with the department chairs in each building. These chairpersons and you have agreed that the curriculum in the four major subjects (English, math, science, and social studies) needs to be reviewed. The committee has agreed that by June each curriculum department is to begin a self-study of its curriculum's scope and sequence. Four months into the project, you find that the chair of the mathematics department at the high school has done nothing toward completing the task.

Listed here are the five advantages of reaching a settlement that you could use to put pressure on this chairperson. For each advantage, write how you would use it to move this person toward completing the task. After finishing this section, review your responses and choose the approach that you feel has the best opportunity of succeeding. Explain your answer.

1. Relationship _____

_____

2. Cost _____

_____

3. Stress _____

_____

4. Time _____

_____

5. BATNA _____

_____

Which advantage would you choose to use, and why?

_____

_____

_____

_____

---

meant to be threats. Rather, they are things you can do that make the other party less comfortable remaining in the position of not wanting to reach a settlement. Many of these things might happen naturally if the period of nonsettlement lasts too long, but it may be in your interests to hasten the process.

Provide a Face-to-Face Encounter

It is easy to postpone negotiations if the parties are at a distance from each other. This is especially true if there is a mediator whom both parties respect and admire. The two sides can deal with each other only through the third party without ever feeling pressure to settle. A striking example of this is seen in the various conflicts in the Middle East. U.S. secretaries of state over the past several administrations have carried on shuttle diplomacy, with little success. The main parties, however, have never met face to face to talk about the issues. Using the secretary of state as mediator, they have managed to hold off an agreement. The one exception to this occurred when President Jimmy Carter asked the heads of state of Israel and Egypt to meet face to face at Camp David. At this encounter, pressure was successfully exerted for them to reach an accord.

In a school building, additional pressure is exerted if the principal can manage to bring together all the parties in a dispute. For example, suppose a parent calls to complain about some action of a teacher. After investigating, the principal finds that the action needs to cease and explains this to the teacher. Nevertheless, the action continues. At this point it would be wise to bring the teacher and the parent together. This face-to-face meeting puts pressure on the two disputants and forces them to reach some resolution. The principal is no longer the go between, and the two parties cannot ignore each other. As another example—one every principal knows well—it is one thing to get a call from the superintendent about a matter and quite another to be told to report to his or her office to discuss the issue.

Overload the Circuits

If one party is stalling, another way to bring pressure is to swamp the person with detailed explanations, lengthy memos, bundles of data to be analyzed, long telephone conversations, frequent meetings with others, specific and complex inquiries for data, and other demands on the person's time. The stalling disputant will come to feel the inconvenience of not settling and may decide that his or her time and energy could be better used elsewhere. This is especially true if the other party realizes that you are not going to give up and go away too soon.

For example, take the case of the junior high and high school principals given the task of deciding which high school teacher will be transferred to the junior high. The reason for the transfer is a declining enrollment at the high school level and an increasing enrollment in the junior high. Naturally, no principal wants to give up staff, so the high school principal stalls. To exert pressure for settlement, the junior high principal schedules two meetings a week with the high school principal. Between meetings, memos and data analyses on class sizes and master schedules are requested and sent. The junior high principal asks the assistant superintendent to attend a few of the meetings. Finally, faced with the prospect of a Saturday meeting, the high school principal offers two choices of staff members for transfer.

Use Peer Pressure

In this situation, you muster the support of the other party's peers to exert pressure. These people may not take any direct action to confront their colleague, but they may decide not to support the person, either. This lack of support amounts to pressure. Sometimes you need to go directly to the people being represented by the recalcitrant person and explain the situation. By providing facts and clarifying the interests at hand, you are giving these individuals enough information to make an independent decision. They may decide that it is in their own best interests to explore ways to settle the conflict.

Worsen the Other's BATNA

If you know the other party's BATNA, you can take steps to make it an unattractive option. Once this fallback position loses its luster, the other party may decide that it is time to look for other options for settlement. There is the story of the parent of a special education student who refused to allow her child to be placed in a mainstream class. Instead, she wanted the committee on special education to place the student in a private school on the other side of the county. She refused to sign any Individualized Education Plan that did not have this specific recommendation. Her BATNA was that the committee would have to provide a teacher at home until her daughter was placed in this special school. The chairman of the committee was frustrated because he knew this child could be placed appropriately in a special education class in a local building. He decided to take the student's records to this private school and, after a long talk with its director, he convinced the director that the student would not be appropriately placed in the private school. Once informed of this rejection, the mother, realizing her BATNA was not a long-term solution, went back to the committee ready to negotiate the child's placement.

Activities 4-2 and 4-3 will give you some practice in deciding how to use pressure to move a conflict toward resolution.

ACTIVITY 4-2

The PTA president of one of the elementary schools in your district has called you to complain about the PTA's fund-raising activities in one of the middle schools in the district. Apparently, both PTAs are using the same material to raise money and therefore are in conflict. The PTA presidents of both schools have asked you, as superintendent, to help them settle the difficulty. You have met with both presidents for over three hours, but there does not seem to be any way of reaching an agreement to settle the conflict.

Four ways of applying additional pressure to settle a conflict are listed here. Write what you would do, using each method, to help these PTA presidents reach an agreement. After reviewing your responses, choose the one method you would use to settle this conflict. Why would you choose this one?

1. Face-to-face encounter _____

_____

2. Overloading circuits _____

_____

3. Using peer pressure _____

_____

4. Worsening the other's BATNA _____

_____

Which method would you choose to settle this conflict, and why?

_____

_____

_____

_____

ACTIVITY 4-3

Listed here are a number of situations that require you to choose one of the methods discussed previously to exert pressure on the other party to reach a settlement of a particular conflict. After reading about each situation, write down how you would use one of the pressure points. Compare your response to those recorded at the end of this worksheet.

1. Your friend, who is also chair of the social studies department, has been lax in keeping track of the budget supply items. Double orders have been received, and invoices for books have been lost. Payments to vendors are delayed. You have discussed the situation with your friend, and you both agree that things are a mess. In calling him into your office, you plan to exert pressure on your friend to clean up the budget backlog. How would you do this?

_____

_____

_____

_____

2. One of the building principals is known to disagree with you, the assistant superintendent, on the issue of allowing parent representation on building-level committees. You both have explained your positions in the situation and understand where the other person is coming from. The principal, at the moment, has not changed, despite a promise that some committee at some future time will have a parent as a member. You are impatient with the ambiguity of this promise. You feel a need to exert pressure on her to settle this conflict by appointing parents to a committee soon. How would you do this?

_____

_____

_____

_____

3. One teaching aide on your staff has called in sick on the third Friday in December for the last three years. You have discussed the facts with him and would like to know what is going on. He refuses to talk about it and claims that he is within his contractual right to take a sick day whenever he chooses. He is correct on this point. You cannot deny him a sick day if he calls in sick and has days remaining in his sick bank. He becomes irate and claims that if his union president knew about this, he would file a grievance on the issue of harassment. You cannot afford to let this conflict end with a threat.

You need to exert pressure on the aide to continue talking to you about the issue and your interests. How would you exert this pressure?

_____

_____

_____

Suggested Responses

1. Cite the relationship you have with your friend. Talk about what the two of you share outside of work and how important that is to you. Ask him to get more involved and stay on top of his budget as a favor to you. If necessary, cite some things you have done for him as part of the friendship.

2. Cite the time it has taken to resolve the issue of putting a parent on a committee. Inform the principal that by the following Friday you would like the names of two parents who have volunteered to serve on a committee. On the Thursday before the due date, have your secretary—not you—call the principal to find out who the parents are. By having your secretary call, you are informing the principal that the issue is not one you are going to discuss any more but one on which you require action. By calling on Thursday, you are exerting additional time pressure by reminding the principal of her task. If the task is not yet done, the principal can respond that she has until Friday, but she will realize that she should get on with the task. If the parents have already been contacted, the secretary will get the names.

3. You need to intensify the pressure here to have the aide keep talking with you and settle the conflict. Provide a face-to-face encounter involving the aide, the union president, and you. Most union presidents are concerned that members not abuse the contract. Clearly, this aide is taking advantage of the contract and, in the process, has the potential to hurt other members' benefits in future contracts. In a face-to-face meeting, you can stack the deck against the aide and put pressure on him to keep talking to you and perhaps change his ways.

MICHAEL'S CONFLICT ▪▪▪▪▪▪▪▪▪▪▪▪

Moving Michael's parents and the English teacher to reach a settlement was accomplished using two of the skills mentioned in this chapter. The first tactic was overloading the circuits, and the second was the use of time. By focusing on the record that the Jameses had brought, the principal attempted to have all the parties examine this record in detail. The Jameses claimed that their son had failed to complete only one assignment and that the other two were completed and in his locker. They also said that the grades Mr. Fritz had given Michael were not appropriate for the work already handed in. Acting as a fact-finder, the principal went back and forth between the teacher and the parents, clarifying the facts. The discussion centered on who had what, and when they had it. This process was as much one of clarifying the data as one of defining the problem. The English teacher was the first to feel the pressure of spending so much time on this detailed list of reports. Finally, he was willing to drop his positional bargaining and make a concession.

To make use of the time factor, the principal, aware that in fifteen minutes the teacher had to get to class, announced to the parents that everyone needed to work quickly to determine the facts because the teacher was ready to leave. Notice that the principal did *not* say that everyone needed to work quickly to reach a settlement. This would have been a presumptuous statement because neither party was interested at this point in settling outside their respective positional statements. But when the principal raised the issue of time, the parents also said they both had to get to work. In this way time became a silent factor, which the principal used to his advantage.

As was mentioned in Chapter Two, the decision was made to keep the English teacher out of the direct discussions because of the hostility expressed earlier. This face-to-face encounter would have increased the pressure beyond the limit. Most likely, tempers would have flared and everyone would have demonstrated anger. But once the English teacher had made a concession and the parents had rejected it, the way was open for the principal to offer a solution to the conflict. At this point, both the teacher and the parents were feeling pressure to end the conflict. The move toward settlement had begun.

TACTIC 4: FINDING WAYS TO SETTLE

The purpose of the skills discussed in this section is to formulate settlement options that the participants can use. By now, the parties to the conflict should be ready to consider settlement, but they probably doubt whether they can trust each other and whether they will gain a resolution that will satisfy their demands. Most likely they still have demands or positions, and they may make statements to this effect. If they came to the meeting angry, they probably are still hurt and, despite their disengagement from angry demonstrations, will probably have a flare-up now and then. In general, however, the parties are focused on searching for a joint gain and are relatively trustful at this point that this can be achieved. If they feel that joint gains will dissolve, they will revert to their earlier positional statements.

The discussion of this tactic is divided into two parts: how to search for conflicting interests and how to search for common interests. Included in the discussion are examples of process techniques you can use to facilitate a quick conclusion to the search.

Exploring Conflicting Interests

Most negotiators go into resolution meetings searching for the common ground, those issues on which all parties can readily agree. The purpose is clear: to generate a rapid resolution process, which will set the tone for tackling the more controversial issues. There is nothing wrong with this strategy, and it often works. The richest rewards of settlement, however, can come from another area: conflicting interests.

Most negotiators shy away from this area out of fear of generating renewed conflict. This is a valid fear. However, if the participants in the dispute are honestly interested in a joint-gain settlement, then searching for settlement options amid the conflicting interests can be a rewarding process. The energy that drives the conflict can be harnessed to drive the settlement. Once they get into this area, the participants will find themselves dissecting the conflict among competing interests and using the energy that brought them to the table to reach a resolution and walk away from the table.

How is this done? The key is to have all participants list which of the items being negotiated are of prime importance to them. Then ask them to list those items that are of little or no interest to them. All parties then look at these lists to see if any of the items have contrasting values. For instance, does the item of prime interest for the first party have no value to the second, and vice versa? There are many areas in which this type of analysis can be done: time, possessions, risk, forecast resources, and interest. The differences that may exist for conflicting interest and risk will be discussed. For further discussion of this topic, see *The Manager as Negotiator* by David A. Lax and James K. Sebenius (New York: Free Press, 1986).

Conflict of Interest

An example of this type of difference can be illustrated in the conflict that emerged when an assistant superintendent gave the middle school principal and the high school principal the task of deciding which full-time foreign language teacher from the middle school would have to be shared with the high school for the coming school year. Despite the declining enrollment at the middle school, the principal had no desire to lose one of his teachers. His position was that he could not lose the teacher because it would destroy the middle school organization, which was based on teams. The high school principal's position was that his school had large class sizes in the foreign language classes and needed to offer more sections of French.

When they started to analyze their differences, it became apparent to both principals that a solution could be worked out. The answer lay in their differing values. Here is how they broke these values apart.

MIDDLE SCHOOL
Value: Need to preserve the team organization of the school
Nonvalue: Need for a full-time foreign language teacher (because of a decline in enrollment)

HIGH SCHOOL
Value: Need for three sections of a foreign language teacher
Nonvalue: Need for a French language teacher specifically. Any foreign language teacher would do because the daily schedule of the personnel in the foreign language department could be adjusted to accommodate the high class enrollments in French language classes.

The resolution of this conflict lay in the fact that what was of highest value to the high school, namely the need for three sections of any foreign language teacher, was a nonvalue to the middle school as long as the team structure could be kept intact. This team structure in turn was a nonvalue for the high school. The settlement took the form that the middle school would develop its schedule and use its foreign language sections and its other special subject areas to support the team structure. At the end of this process, the middle school would adjust the special sections to allow for three sections of foreign language to be freed up for the high school.

The high school agreed to take the three sections of a language teacher whenever the middle school could free the teacher. As it turned out, these sections were found in the morning. The schedule could be arranged so that the teacher could start teaching at the high school before the middle school even started its day and still be available to come back to the middle school and fit into the schedule of one of the school's seventh-grade teams.

Activity 4-4 illustrates the resolution of a conflict of interest.

ACTIVITY 4-4

To illustrate how a conflicting sense of interest opens up possibilities of choice, you will be asked in this activity to make a critical decision involving value. A parent group in your district has asked that more students be allowed to participate in the elementary-level gifted and talented program. As assistant superintendent in charge of this area, you must make a choice.

1. Expand the program at the school by increasing the enrichment level courses. The program will become less elite and the standards will drop, but more students will enroll.

or

2. Develop a gifted class for the brightest students and a pull-out gifted development program for other bright students.

or

3. Plan on expanding the pull-out gifted program so that more students can have the opportunity to enter this program.

Your choice: _____

Reasons for your choice.

_____

_____

_____

There are no right or wrong answers to this decision. The choice depends on your situation. The process illustrates how conflicting values can lead to alternative bargaining options.

Conflicting Risk

Often, participants in a conflict have different views about taking risks. Some are willing to gamble that things will work out in the future. This view may be based on a generally positive attitude, on a sense of how people and things work, or on past experience. Others take fewer risks because they have more to lose, are not as trusting of the process, or are more pessimistic in general about how things will turn out. There is evidence that individuals treat risks concerning gains as different from risks concerning loses. People will risk more if there are gains to be made than they will if they might lose what they already have. In either case, these differing views can be exploited to search for a joint gain.

One principal was confronted by the parents of a student entering the third grade. They demanded that their child be placed in the gifted program. The principal met with the child's teacher, who felt that the child was indeed very bright but was not mature enough to handle the responsibility associated with the gifted class. The teacher felt the child needed more time to develop social skills and that the academic challenge could wait. The parents made a position statement that their child must be placed in a gifted program or they would go to the board of education. Upon analysis, the values and nonvalues of the participants looked like this:

PRINCIPAL

Value: The total development of the child

Nonvalue: Whether the child will enter the gifted program in the future

PARENTS

Value: That their child be given the opportunity to be challenged and perform work that is equal to her ability

Nonvalue: Who teaches the gifted program or when or where it meets

The value for the principal—that the child be given the opportunity to develop as a total person—is not a value considered by the parents at this point. The value for the parents—that the child be challenged or that she perform work that is equal to her ability—is not a value to the principal at this point. The principal knows that the child is bright and will eventually do very well in a gifted program, but he is willing to risk not placing the child in a gifted program now so that her social needs can be fulfilled. His experience and knowledge of child development tell him that this is a good risk. The parents are afraid that if their child is denied the gifted program, she will not reach her full academic potential or will even regress. They have not considered the social development factor raised by the principal. At this point they are confused as to whether they should place the social maturation of their daughter ahead of her intellectual growth. They also wonder if not placing her in a gifted program now might put her at risk of never making it into such a program.

The conflict over risk can be exploited here to reach a settlement. The risk needs to be shifted to the party who is not afraid of risk, in this case the principal. He offers an option of joint gain based on the following settlement: The child will not enter the gifted program this school year. However, the teacher, with the parents' help, will develop some common strategies that will help the child in her social development. Her progress will be monitored for the duration of the school year. The child, barring unforseen circumstances, will be allowed to enter the gifted program at the beginning of the fourth grade.

This settlement transfers to the principal the risk that the child may not be ready for the program next year. It is a weighted risk because the principal knows from experience that this type of child will grow over the year and will be ready. The parents do not have to risk anything. Of course, they do not want to, because they are dealing with their child's life. They would rather have a guarantee of success in the future grade than a doubt about their child's success in the present grade.

Activity 4-5 deals with the role of risk in conflict resolution.

Exploring Common Interests

It is easy to locate common interests: They are the interests most participants in a dispute are verbalizing. It takes only a small extra step to link the interests of the individual participants and make them joint interests. Areas of common interest are often found in process issues, relationship issues, time factors, shared principles, and cost issues. All of these, alone and in combination, can be used to forge a settlement. A few of these interests will be discussed here.

ACTIVITY 4-5

To illustrate how a conflicting sense of risk opens up possibilities of choice, you will be asked to make a critical decision involving the dimension of risk. Your school board has recommended to you, the superintendent, the implementation of a district-wide computer program. Given the three choices that follow, which would you do?

1. Install the recommended $50,000 computer lab in a building, and encourage teachers to attend the workshops to use the equipment and software.

or

2. For the first year, offer computer training workshops. Determine the level of interest. In the second year, add the $50,000 computer lab.

or

3. Encourage teachers to attend regional computer training programs. As each teacher attends these workshops, add a computer to that teacher's classroom.

Your choice: _____

Reasons for your choice:

_____

_____

_____

_____

    There is no one right or wrong choice. The value you hold to be the most important—the prime value—is the one for which you will choose to bargain hard.

Common Process

In the course of trying to find a solution to a conflict, a lot of time, effort, cost, and concessions are involved. All the participants have a vested interest in keeping the process rolling toward final settlement. Often there is an expectation that things will change and that the conflict will be resolved, not only by the direct participants but also by those parties associated with each side of the issue. A parent trying to advocate for a better grade from a teacher has raised, by her mere presence in the school, the expectation that her son will get a better grade or else the teacher will receive a reprimand. With this kind of expectation, it is difficult for the mother to leave with an unresolved conflict. In cases like this, it is often wise to agree to continue talking or to continue the process rather than admit defeat.

Common Relationship

Interests in this area rest with the need of the participants to be able to work with one another once the conflict is over. Many participants in a conflict have a future working relationship to worry about. You cannot maintain an ongoing conflict or demonstrate outbursts of anger with someone with whom you have to work on other issues. You have a common interest in preserving the relationship.

A parent who gets angry with a teacher's action can walk away from a conflict meeting with a teacher without the fear of destroying a relationship because that parent can always demand that his or her child be transferred out of the class. This is a common occurrence. It is rare, however, for a parent to leave a conflict with a principal unresolved, because it is assumed that that parent's child will be in that school for a few years. The parent and the principal have a mutual need for a positive working relationship. The same is true of a principal and a teacher. Neither a teacher nor a principal can afford to stay angry with the other for a long period. The educational environment of the teacher's classroom could erode without the mutual support that a teacher and principal offer each other.

Common Principle

In many schools it is possible to generate a common vision or common mission that binds people together. Conflicts need to be resolved with joint gains because the opposing parties are linked by a common idea, symbol, or feeling about the school, its students, or its community. For example, two teachers in conflict over whether a student should leave class to attend remedial reading may look at the school's mission statement to determine what is good for the child rather than what is good for the individual teachers involved.

Consider the fate of the principal who could not get the staff to develop a value statement about the school because no one wanted to take the time to work on it. Rather than approaching the task as a chore to be done, she decided to view it as a need to pull the staff together. When the staff saw the task as a common good, the principal had no problem getting volunteers to work on it.

Activity 4-6 gives you an opportunity to make decisions about your prime values in the process of resolving a conflict.

ACTIVITY 4-6

This worksheet gives you the opportunity to apply Tactic 4 in other areas of opportunity. For each of two different situations, you will be given three choices and asked to make a value decision on the basis of whatever is of prime value to you, the value for which you will negotiate. The remaining two choices are nonvalues, which you would be willing to give up in order to gain your prime value. The decisions involve common areas school administrators deal with—time and resources. After each decision, mark your choice.

TIME

This choice involves the dimension of time. Your superintendent has charged you with improving test scores in your sixth-grade reading program. Of the three possible choices listed here, which would you choose?

1. You can introduce a reading program that will increase test scores 12 percent over last year's scores, but you run the risk the increase may not be sustained the following year.

or

2. You can introduce a teacher training program that will increase test scores 3 percent each year for four consecutive years. This increase is gradual, but it will not erode.

or

3. You can introduce a new program and teacher training that will increase test scores 10 percent over last year's, with a very low risk that the scores would decline over the next few years.

Your choice is: _____

The reason for your choice:

_____

_____

_____

There are no right or wrong choices. For each person, the choice depends on what value is most important to you at a particular time and place. In a negotiation process, you would use this choice as your prime value; you would bargain hard for this choice.

RESOURCES

This dimension involves making a decision about how to provide guidance counselor resources. As a building principal, you have been given funds to hire an additional guidance counselor for the next year. The students in your school have many needs. Which need should you address when you hire the guidance counselor?

1. You should hire a drug/alcohol abuse counselor because the teachers have been reporting an increase in substance abuse among students.

or

2. You should hire a career/college placement counselor because that is what your PTA is requesting.

or

3. Your special education population is increasing, so you should hire a counselor with a background in handling emotional problems.

Your choice is: _____

The reason for your choice:

_____

_____

_____

As in the previous exercises, there are no right or wrong answers. What is important is that you see the value in exploring conflicting interests about an issue. Out of these interests, a settlement option often will emerge.

How to Develop Options

Whether the participants are generating options from conflicting interests or from common interests, some procedure needs to be developed for doing this. How do the ideas emerge? Listed here are a number of different procedures you can use for this task. They are not mutually exclusive, nor is this list exhaustive.

Brainstorming

This is a procedure known to all administrators. Though used often, it generally goes unnoticed by the participants in a dispute. Like all good negotiating skills, process skills should not be noticeable. What is important is the final settlement. Nevertheless, it is important to review brainstorming as a skill here because it can be used in a number of different ways and can be incorporated easily into any of the other skills listed here.

Brainstorming is the process whereby people list in any fashion any number of ideas that they feel may be either conflicting or common issues. At first, the ideas proposed are just listed. It is valuable to have the list of ideas visible to all during the process. The first step, then, is simply to list a number of ideas that might work. The second step is to invite comments about the various ideas. There should be no discussion of the proposed ideas until everyone at the meeting has had an opportunity to offer an idea. The point of brainstorming is to encourage ideas to come forth, and commenting on them may discourage some people from subjecting their ideas to public judgment or possibly to personal attack. Another reason not to evaluate each idea in turn is that it breaks the momentum generated by the thinking process. During brainstorming, ideas are often linked to other ideas, and momentum is needed for this to happen.

Brainstorming can be used in any number of creative ways. All the participants can work together in the brainstorming and the list can be generated from a group effort. Or each person can make a list on a piece of paper and hand it to one person, who then writes down everyone's ideas. Then, with the whole group back together, further ideas can be generated from individuals in the group. People from the opposing sides can be mixed together in subgroups for the purpose of brainstorming. This blending should reduce the need for each person to echo his or her side's "party line." More creative brainstorming may occur in subgroups than is permitted by the dynamics of the large-group process.

Discussion Groups

Some conflicts involve so many different groups of people that it is necessary to allow only a large representative group to be involved in the settlement process. This may be particularly true in school buildings and with issues that are faced by an entire staff. Discussion groups can build trust in the process because everyone has an equal opportunity to be involved. These groups allow for the use of staff knowledge and experience. They decentralize the process of reaching a decision by giving every person the chance to become involved. Most important, they build unity and strengthen morale in the conflict resolution group. The process toward settlement becomes a cooperative venture, not a competition or a confrontation.

The following procedures are important to use in providing for a group discussion of the settlement options. For further clarification, see *Effective Group Problem Solving* by William M. Fox (San Francisco: Jossey-Bass, 1987).

1. *Define the purpose of the group.* The people involved need to know what they are doing. Are they present to define conflicting issues, common issues, or both? Is their task to analyze each of these issues according to value and nonvalue? Or perhaps their task is first to determine if all the participants in the dispute are represented, or to discover and analyze data and information about the problem.

2. *Gather some of the input before the meeting.* This is important because group discussions can be an endless process. It is both economically sound and humanly more efficient if some data are collected or a survey given before the group assembles.

3. *All information gathered about the conflict should be shared with all participants.* Some administrators may feel that the data will swamp the staff. It is better to swamp them, however, than to give them only half the picture. A guided discussion of the data will allow the participants to sort out what is important and what is not. It is important to have a discussion on all the data and information gathered.

4. *Permit any single objection from any individual to block the generation of an idea.* If you remember that a feeling of joint gain is important to a resolution, then it is important to say at this stage of the process that if anyone objects to an analysis, the analysis will be thrown out. One way of moving beyond an objection is to give the objector more information, which could clarify the objector's reasons for blocking an option.

5. *Provide for voting on each issue.* Voting should be anonymous because no matter how close the group has become, you need to make sure that everyone has "bought" the option to settle. Those issues that still have clarification problems can be tabled until a second discussion and then voted on again. The process should be an informative one and, through information gathering and active discussion, the issues should become clear enough that participants can agree or disagree with them.

Activity 4-7 shows in outline format how two or more groups can work constructively on a problem at the same time.

ACTIVITY 4-7

Use this outline format when two or more groups are working on a problem at the same time and providing feedback to each other.

GROUP 1

Summary of discussions and main ideas:

_____

_____

_____

_____

Tasks assigned:

_____ (Name of person)

_____ (Name of person)

    This summary and task assignment should be copied and given to members of all working groups.

GROUP 2

Summary of discussions and main ideas:

_____

_____

_____

_____

Tasks assigned:

_____ (Name of person)

_____ (Name of person)

This summary and task assignment should be copied and given to members of all working groups. Once the members have discussed the summaries and the individuals have reported on their specific assignments, the whole group or the joint groups should meet or send a representative to develop a common draft. This draft can be in a format similar to the one described here.

Mediation

Another way to generate ideas is to use a mediator. Our ongoing case of Michael is a good illustration of how a school administrator can be used as an effective mediator. Mediation is an extension of the negotiation process. It allows a third party, or a group of individuals collectively representing a third party, to become the facilitators of the dispute. The decision-making power still rests with those directly involved. The mediator is called in when the parties involved in the dispute feel they cannot settle the conflict themselves. The mediator has many functions. A few of them are listed here.

1. *The chairperson:* In this capacity the mediator organizes the meeting agenda and procedures, and often initiates and runs the meetings as well. In this leadership position, the mediator moves the process along by offering procedural or settlement suggestions.

2. *The facilitator:* As facilitator, the mediator moves the resolution process along by keeping the parties communicating with one another. He or she clarifies issues, sums up points of view, and generally tries to keep the rules of effective communication intact. The mediator offers reassurance to individuals when needed and challenges blockers when necessary.

3. *A resource:* Often, individuals not involved in a conflict need to be brought into the meetings. Their expertise or other qualities may be essential for reaching settlement. Mediators may know how to collect data, organize it, and present it clearly to all parties. At other times, their knowledge of outside resources can be used to help facilitate the information acquisition needed to settle the dispute.

4. *A scapegoat:* Mediating a dispute can be a difficult role because either of the disputing parties may view the mediator as siding with the other party. Principals who play the mediator's role are viewed with suspicion by everyone. In a parent–teacher conflict, the principal is seen by the parent as siding with the teachers and by the teachers as siding with the parent. Similarly, in a teacher–superintendent of schools conflict, the principal is viewed by the teachers as siding with the administration and by the superintendent as siding with the teachers.

A mediator needs to know when it is necessary to hold separate caucuses with the parties. In deciding to hold separate meetings, the mediator should judge whether there are clear advantages to doing so. Caucusing can be an effective way to move the resolution process along. If the mediator feels that the parties would share feelings, talk about settlement proposals, and share information in front of a neutral party better than they do in the presence of the other conflict participants, then setting up a caucus can be advantageous. Sometimes a mediator needs to confront one of the parties about an unreasonable stance, confrontational behavior, or lack of planning. To do so in front of everyone would embarrass and probably upset the confronted party. Rather than for the mediator to appear to be taking sides, it is wiser for such a confrontation to take place in private. Caucuses also give the parties in a dispute time to reflect on the resolution process. In a caucus, the participants do not have to think and act at the same time. A period of withdrawal to assess progress, generate options, and design tactics to seek settlement can be useful.

An excellent resource on the roles and functions of a mediator is *The Mediation Process* by Christopher W. Moore (San Francisco: Jossey-Bass, 1987). Activity 4-8 is designed to give you practice in identifying an appropriate mediator for a conflict.

Role Playing

Participants in a conflict can use role playing to propose hypothetical solutions to the conflict through a series of "what if's." Administrators can use their administrative team to test ideas that might work to resolve the situation. In some districts, it is not uncommon for the principal to meet with a trusted teacher or, if the teachers' union representative is willing, to use role playing to develop strategies for working with a teacher who is performing below par. Testing the waters in this way gives the administrator some feedback on the reasonableness of the settlement option.

One district in California had to announce to its teaching staff

---

ACTIVITY 4-8

In identifying a mediator, use this worksheet to help choose the most appropriate candidate. In the spaces that follow, write the name of the person on your staff you feel can best fulfill the desired characteristic. Explain your choices.

Unbiased _____

Knowledgeable about the issue _____

Experienced with the problem _____

Discreet _____

If a person meets more than one of these criteria, then you have the possibility of a good mediator. This person should be approached and asked to serve in that role. Ideally, both parties to the conflict should be involved in this process. That is, both should seek out a person they feel can mediate the dispute. Once this process is complete, the two parties should sit down and select one of the chosen individuals to serve as a mediator.

---

that the district was going to be absorbed into a much larger neighboring school district. This move was the result of extensive negotiating, and the teachers were well aware that such a proposal might be made. In preparing to make the announcement, the superintendent of schools expected to face a hostile crowd, and the principals confirmed the fact that some teachers planned to speak out strongly against the move. The superintendent asked the administrative council to role-play the various positions teachers might take on this move. Through a series of role-playing exercises and discussion of the effects, the superintendent refined a number of options that he would offer to the teachers to make the move less disruptive. The superintendent went to the meeting with greater confidence about the outcome and with a few proposals to offer the teachers so that they could reach a positive settlement.

Outside Resources

A mediator can serve as an outside resource. Other people who may help the parties generate settlement options could be experts in law, psychology, curriculum, management, or child advocacy.

The chief difficulty with proposals from resources outside the direct conflict is that they bear the "NIH" ("Not Invented Here") symbol. Proposals that do not come from the participants themselves do not promote a feeling of ownership. The parties to the dispute need to have an interest in these proposals if they are going to be made part of the settlement. Unfortunately for many outside resources, although their proposals are good, the fact that they had to come from an outside source is enough to deter their acceptance. Therefore, it is best to use outside resources for information-gathering tasks that can then provide input for all the participants to use in generating their own solutions.

Arbitration

The final method of reaching settlement is for the parties to surrender their settlement options to the hands of an arbitrator. Here, the parties consent to follow the settlement generated by the arbitrator rather than produce one themselves. This often happens when the parties feel they are at an impasse or when there is a tremendous amount of hostility involved.

The problem associated with any settlement generated by arbitration is that the arbitrator usually "splits the difference" in any dispute. The participants, knowing this, tend to present extreme demands or exaggerate their situation in front of the arbitrator. They resist making any concessions so as not to show the arbitrator that they are softening in their demands. Therefore, arbitration is bound to present a somewhat contrived settlement.

One way to encourage participants to settle a dispute themselves is to devise a strategy whereby, if the case goes to arbitration, each of the two parties involved in the case must present to the arbitrator a complete final settlement option. The arbitrator can choose only one of the two complete settlement proposals. This strategy forces the participants to offer their own concessions and to search actively for settlement options. In this case, the prospect of going to the arbitrator is dreadful because of the extent of the loss one of the two parties will incur.

Activity 4-9 gives you some practice in designing a settlement option to present to an arbitrator.

SUMMARY

The third tactic focused on the need to exert pressure on the participants in a conflict to get them to move toward settlement. The advantages of settlement include the factors of existing relation-

ACTIVITY 4-9

Before you go to an arbitrator, you should have a clear, well-planned proposal for settlement. You should also have a clear idea of what you will lose if the arbitrator decides against you. In the space given here, write out what you think would be your offer to the arbitrator if asked.

What would happen? _____

_____

Who would do it? _____

_____

How would you expect it to be done? _____

_____

How would you know it was done? _____

_____

When would you expect it done? _____

_____

On the other side of the coin, if the arbitrator ruled against you, what would be the worst thing or things that would happen? In the following space, write out what you think would happen if you lost the decision.

New things not achieved: _____

_____

Things lost that were in place before: _____

_____

Time or energy investment lost: _____

_____

Monetary loss: _____

_____

Personnel loss: _____

_____

Reputation loss: _____

_____

ships; the costs, stress, and time involved; and the use of BATNAs. Ways to intensify the pressure to settle include using face-to-face encounters, overloading the circuits, bringing peer pressure to bear, and worsening others' BATNAs. The use of threats as a tactic was discouraged.

Once the parties have agreed to search for settlement options, they need to take a long, hard look at their interests associated with the conflict. The fourth tactic described how this process can be accomplished. A number of methods for using the conflicting interests or values of the different parties to find a settlement option were described. In addition, common interests among the parties, in areas such as relationships and basic principles, were described as other ways to generate a settlement. Throughout the chapter you are encouraged to look at the relative value or nonvalue of each interest involved in the dispute. A number of option-generating procedures were described: brainstorming, discussion groups, mediation, role playing, the use of outside resources, and arbitration.

MICHAEL'S CONFLICT

Michael's parents were now ready to reach a settlement. The issue of Michael's future was decided by the English teacher's concession that he did not want Michael back in his classroom. That was a position identical to that of the parents, and it did not conflict with the principal's interests. Michael could be transferred to another English teacher's class.

The conflict that remained was focused on the grade Michael should receive for his first quarter's work. The teacher was sticking to his demand that the F remain. The parents wanted their son to receive a better grade because of the circumstances surrounding Michael's failure to complete his work and because they felt the teacher was biased. The principal, after analyzing the problem and considering the teacher's concession, decided to generate an option for settlement based on the parties' conflicting values in time. Broken down into values and nonvalues, the situation looked like this. (Keep in mind that the principal, acting as a mediator, has assumed leadership of this meeting and is now proposing a settlement based on the interests of the parents and also on those of the school, which he represents.)

PARENTS

Value: That Michael be removed from Mr. Fritz's English class

Nonvalue: The grades Michael will receive from his new English teacher

TEACHER

Value: That he be allowed the freedom to grade

Nonvalue: Michael's final grade

SCHOOL

Values: That Michael acquire an understanding of this curriculum, and that the grading process of the school be kept intact

Nonvalue: How long it takes Michael to acquire an understanding of the curriculum

The resolution of this conflict was achieved by blending the values of the parents, the teacher, and the school. At the moment, no party has as a value Michael's grades in the future. This common nonvalue was also used to build a settlement option.

The form of this option, proposed by the principal in the mediator's role, was that Michael would be removed from Mr. Fritz's class (parents' value) but that the first quarter's grade of F would remain on the report card (teacher's value). However, the next three grades Michael would receive from his new English teacher would be based solely on the work he did in his new class. In averaging the final grade in June, which typically would reflect work done throughout the year, the teacher would average only these three grades rather than all four. The F grade would be excluded. However, Michael would be required to complete parts of the first quarter's work for the new teacher because she teaches the course curriculum in a different sequence than Mr. Fritz does. Therefore, Michael would be required to relearn parts of the first-quarter work and also to catch up on the work his new class had already completed (school's value).

This proposal reflected the interest of the parents that Michael be removed from Mr. Fritz's class, the interest of Mr. Fritz that he be allowed to grade as he judged, and the interest of the school that Michael gain an understanding of the curriculum. The form this final settlement package took will be seen in the discussion of the final tactic employed.

SUGGESTED READINGS

Blumberg, Arthur. (1985). *The School Superintendent: Living with Conflict.* New York: Columbia University Press, Teacher's College.

Fox, William M. (1987). *Effective Group Problem Solving.* San Francisco: Jossey-Bass.

Lax, David A., & Sebenius, James K. (1986). *The Manager as Negotiator.* New York: The Free Press.

Lieberman, Ann. (1988, February). "Expanding the Leadership Team." *Educational Leadership, 45,* 4–8.

Moore, Christopher W. (1986). *The Mediation Process: Practical Strategies for Resolving Conflict.* San Francisco: Jossey-Bass.

Neale, Margaret A., Bazerman, Max H. (1985). "Effects of Framing and Negotiator Overconfidence on Bargaining Behaviors and Outcomes." *Academy of Management Journal, 28,* 34–49.

Pruitt, D. (1981). *Negotiation Behavior.* New York: Academic Press.

Stulberg, Joseph B. (1987). *Taking Charge/Managing Conflict.* Lexington, MA; Lexington Books.

━━ CONFLICT RESOLUTION GUIDE ━━

Each chapter in this book contains a Conflict Resolution Guide. You can use this guide as a worksheet for any ongoing conflict resolutions in which you are involved. It can serve as a checklist for determining where you are in the resolution process and where you need to go.

    1. After considering the particular conflict list, which pressure point would have the most dramatic impact? Then pick that point to apply and move the negotiations along toward a positive settlement.

PRESSURE POINTS

Relationships _____

Costs _____

Stress _____

Time _____

BATNA _____

INTENSIFYING PRESSURE POINTS

Face-to-face encounters _____

Overload circuits _____

Peer pressure _____

Worsen others' BATNAs _____

    2. Now that a commitment is made, the conflict can be settled by exploring conflicting interests and common interests. Different options can be discovered and/or created by the participants. Six methods to devise settlement options are available.

1. Are there conflicting interests? List values and nonvalues for each of the participants.

    Conflict of interest _____

    _____

    _____

    Conflict of risk _____

    _____

    _____

Conflict of forecast, time, resources, etc. _____

_____

_____

_____

2. Are there common interests? List the values and nonvalues for each of the participants.

_____

_____

_____

_____

_____

   3. Can the values and nonvalues listed here be blended to generate a number of settlement options? Choose one or more of the techniques listed here to generate options.

Brainstorming ideas _____

_____

_____

_____

Discussion group ideas _____

_____

_____

_____

_____

Mediation _____

_____

_____

_____

Role playing _____

_____

Outside resources _____

_____

_____

Arbitration _____

_____

_____

_____

CHAPTER FIVE

Getting What You Want

The process of reaching a conflict resolution has come to its final phase, that of settlement. This phase has as its goal the completion of an agreement on procedures that will bring the original conflict to an end.

Settlement is not like the procedures discussed in the other chapters. It has a different dynamic. Because in using the earlier tactics the participants were searching for common information, avoiding angry outbursts, agreeing to a process of settlement, and agreeing to generate options for settlement, there was a positive expectation of a successful settlement. The potential settlement has the possibility of giving every party involved some new gain, in terms of money, time, recognition, or some other value. Every party involved stands to gain something because of the dynamic whereby the participants have expanded the pie and not just divided a fixed amount of gains.

Now a different dynamic takes over—deciding which participant is to get which piece of the new settlement. Tension arises at this phase because the participants are now moving to capture the gains they have sought or created. Although it is expected that these gains will make all the participants better off, there is a range within which one party will accept some of the gains and feel satisfied, leaving the remainder of the gains for the other party. This range is often referred to as the *zone of agreement*. This chapter is about how to capture or claim these newfound gains without negatively influencing the other participants.

The following diagram illustrates this dynamic more clearly.

Green's   Yellow's
Demand ——————— \————————————————/ ——,———Demand
                            ZONE OF AGREEMENT

At one end is the Green Team's position demand; at the other end is the Yellow Team's position demand. Both are extreme demands, which if either party gains what it wants, will create a losing situation for the other party. After negotiations, the two teams have narrowed their demands to an acceptable zone of agreement. Any settlement within this zone will be better for each team than accepting its BATNA (best alternative to a negotiated agreement) and walking away. Knowing that either team will settle within this zone of the continuum creates a dynamic whereby both teams try to claim as much of the zone of agreement as possible.

The skills described in this chapter—how to shape perceptions, how to propose an option, and how to formalize the agreement—will help you do just that, claim a large piece of the agreement zone.

INFLUENCING WHAT THE OTHER THINKS ABOUT YOU

A teacher was about to see the superintendent of schools to review her negative classroom evaluation. Before the appointment, she decided to call a parent she knew well who was active in the PTA. She also asked the union representative to call the superintendent just before she was due to enter his office and complain about an old clause in the teacher contract. When she arrived at the appointed time, there in the superintendent's office was the PTA spokesperson she had just talked to. Soon after that, the union representative phoned, asking to talk to the superintendent. Even before her meeting began, this teacher had cleverly shaped a perception in the superintendent's eyes. Whether or not these events changed what the superintendent said to her, it is certain that he had to alter his perception of this teacher's influence.

This is what shaping is all about. You are setting the scene for the next phase, choosing an acceptable option. You are trying to influence the other party in such a manner that when you propose an option settlement, an environment exists in which this option can be nourished and grow. Perception can be either subtle or overt, but it is a powerful influence on how we judge facts and make critical decisions. Listed here are a number of areas where this perception can be formed.

Expectation

It is important at this point to emphasize that you are the one who will determine whether you can claim your values. What you do and say, and how, will determine whether or not you gain. You need to assume full responsibility for resolving this conflict in your best interest. You will have to demonstrate to the other party that you are determined and powerful enough to carry off this settlement. You will need to invest your personal and managerial resources to make the settlement take hold and eventually to make it work. To accomplish this, you will need to shape perceptions, choose an option, and formulate the settlement. You will need courage, knowledge, and commitment. In other words, you need to have high expectations for yourself. If you believe you can do it, you are halfway there. People who have doubts about whether they can do it will never accomplish their goals. Negotiation is not so much about the issues as it is about you, the negotiator.

Your high expectations can be translated into the way you frame your opening proposal. In the next section, a variety of ways to make the first proposal will be discussed. Here we are interested in the *what* of the proposal. A number of negotiators claim that toughness, an extreme high opening proposal, a low rate of concessions, and an unyielding posture will result in favorable gains. The chief problem with this tough stance is that although the terms may turn out to be favorable, the final agreements are difficult to hammer out. One reason is that the other party, feeling that it did not get the highest gains in the proposal, wants to be sure it preserves its gains in the written agreement. So this party is more cautious. Another problem with extreme opening proposals is that they often backfire and prompt the other party to present an extreme counteroffer. The result is a deadlock. The other extreme, making a soft opening proposal, will surely result in the other party walking away with most of the gains—not only those in the zone of agreement but most likely even more than that. The ideal opening proposal, then, should be on the tough side, with high expectation for gain, but not sufficiently high to produce a negative reaction from the other party.

Focal Point

It is difficult for the parties in a dispute to come to settlement if they do not have some point on which to focus their discussions. People have trouble dealing with the uncertainty of an option until it is framed in a concrete, specific manner. They need to anchor their negotiations on some point. Your task is to make that anchor point one that is closer to your interests within the zone of agreement. If you can make the starting point of the negotiation on an option a point that you have chosen, the other parties will tend to rally around that point. Negotiations then begin where you want them to. As long as that point is within the zone of agreement, you have an advantage.

There are two keys to using a focal point as a skill. The first is that you need to make the opening offer. This sets the anchor point. If your expectations are high, as discussed previously, then the focal point should be highly in your favor. The exception to this first-out rule will be discussed in the next section, on opening proposals. But for most purposes, being first out is optimum.

The second key is to make the focal point as concrete as possible. It needs to be clear, concise, believable, and memorable. Its image must be the rallying point for your negotiation.

EXAMPLES

Here are two examples of how a focal point can be used to your advantage.

1. In *Trump: The Art of the Deal* (New York: Random House, 1987), Donald Trump describes the final stages of his negotiations with Holiday Inns to develop jointly a new casino in Atlantic City. Trump would provide the building expertise, and Holiday Inns would provide the management skills for the casino operations. This was a true joint gains venture involving millions of dollars. The whole deal depended on a visit the Holiday Inns board of directors was to make to Atlantic City to

view the site proposed for development, after which they would vote on the joint venture. Trump was worried that when the board of directors saw the empty lot, they would not understand the scope of his project. Therefore, he ordered his crew master to round up bulldozers and other heavy equipment and start excavating. He did not care what the crews did, but he wanted them to push the dirt around, and that is just what they did—pushed dirt from one side of the lot to the other, dug holes and filled them up again. The board members were duly impressed. They praised Trump for his ability to get things done. They could see that they needed his building expertise to reach their goals. Trump had set the focal point. When the board met to deliberate, each member had a vivid image of a progressive, zealous partner. The focal point worked, and Trump was on his way.

2. A second example is that of the superintendent of schools who was forced by declining enrollment to close one of her elementary schools. The ad hoc committee that she had formed to study and make a recommendation on this closing went through a difficult process in reaching a decision. When they proposed closing Kennedy School, the superintendent asked the committee to develop a written proposal outlining their findings. Entitled "The Proposal to Close John F. Kennedy Elementary School," the document was offered to the public for deliberation. The superintendent had thereby set the focal point of this controversial decision on the written proposal. When the board of education met to discuss the closing, it referred constantly to the written document. The superintendent was spared the need to stand up and explain the decision to close Kennedy. All she had to do was refer people to the formal written proposal. The arguments pro and con centered on this document, which became the focus of praise and of attack. It had set perception.

Activity 5-1 will give you some practice in setting the focal point.

Limitations

There are real limitations to adopting any option of settlement. Some of these limitations are due to legal, moral, educational, or

---

ACTIVITY 5-1

In setting the focal point, consider how you would handle each of these situations. Write your focal point methodology after each situation.

1. You need to present a proposal for a new project at the next board of education meeting.

   _____

   _____

   _____

2. At your next faculty meeting you need to provide your staff with an overview of how students' test scores have declined.

   _____

   _____

   _____

3. Next month your school or district is being visited by the regional accreditation association.

   _____

   _____

   _____

4. Your staff has reached a conclusion that the students need to set higher expectations for themselves. You have to come up with a plan to help in this process.

   _____

   _____

   _____

financial considerations. Bluntly put, not every good idea can be implemented, at least not right away. Citing the limitations of a settlement option is necessary from the beginning. The other party may not believe that these are real limitations, or it may believe that you are not the person with whom they should be negotiating. But if you believe that there is a limitation, you need to state it.

There is the case of the mother who wanted her daughter on the honor roll because she had achieved an A average. The parent based her calculations on converting the school's letter grades to numerical grades. But she had a conversion chart that differed from the one the school was using. Her chart measured to the nearest tenth place, whereas the school simply calculated the number of As, Bs, Cs, or Ds a student had received. The mother claimed that a numerical average was more precise and therefore a truer measure of her daughter's ability. The school principal explained that the school, being at the elementary level, was not interested in a precise measurement of student ability. Rather, the school measured globally within a range. An A meant that a student was doing excellent work. The mother insisted on a numerical conversion and wanted her daughter placed on the honor roll. The principal cited his limitations in order to put this demand in perspective. He could not unilaterally change the school's grading system, nor could he calculate honor roll status for one student on the basis of a system different from the one used for the other students. He regretted the distress this was causing the mother, but there were limitations on his options.

Artificial limitations are limits the school administrator contrives to foster a sense that some option is or is not feasible. For example, the administrator may instruct his secretary to interrupt him 45 minutes after a meeting has begun to inform him that a parent would like to talk to him. No matter what point the meeting has reached, the principal can expedite the process of reaching a conclusion by citing time limitations. Or a principal may assign the remainder of the meeting to an assistant principal as a way of demonstrating to a party that its demands are so far out of the zone of agreement that they will not be considered until a concession is made. The principal has set a perceptual limitation on the negotiations.

Concessions

In order to reach consensus, the parties to a conflict need to make concessions from their original demands or opening options. How many, how often, and how large should these concessions be? Aside from the fact that concessions alter the content of the proposed option, they also convey a perception of how firm or soft the negotiator can be.

The frequency of making concessions does not seem to matter much. Whether you offer many small concessions or a few large ones will not alter the level of gains you can achieve in the long run. Concessions do, however, produce counter offers and move the negotiations along more quickly to completion. Perhaps this is part of a larger phenomenon of communicating and developing congruence. Needless to say, offering concessions does establish a perception that a settlement can be worked out. It is interesting to note, however, that, when compared to the opening offer, concession making is not as strong an indicator of a positive outcome for a particular negotiator. (See "Enchancing Negotiators' Successfulness" by Stephan Weiss-Wik, *Journal of Conflict Resolution, 27,* 1983, 706–739.) Therefore, the negotiator needs to spend more time developing the opening offer than planning the series of concessions.

Communication

Publicly airing your demands is one way of setting perception. Sometimes this is done to demonstrate to your constituents that you are tough and are truly representing their interests. At other times it is a way of soliciting public support for your position. Or it can be a combination of these two factors. Examples would be President Kennedy's statement in 1961 that the United States was committed to putting a man on the moon by the end of the decade, or quarterback Joe Namath's public "guarantee" of a Super Bowl victory, or more recently candidate George Bush's statement, "Read my lips—no new taxes."

Public announcement of demands, however, can put enormous pressure on the negotiators. They lose their ability to be flexible, to move away from their demands and search for that zone of agreement. This lack of flexibility results in more harm to the constituency than might be expected. An example of how a perception can trap its instigator is seen in the situation in which Henry Kissinger found himself when, in 1972, he announced to the American people that an agreement to end the Vietnam War was at hand when, in fact, he was just beginning to negotiate with the North Vietnamese. This public statement established an expectation among the people; the North Vietnamese then used this public expectation of peace as a form of pressure in order to hold out for more concessions from the United States. Kissinger could not dare to break off negotiations without causing severe repercussions back home. Meanwhile, the other side kept demanding more and more.

Mass communication can also set perception. It is not uncommon for a parent to write a letter to the editor of the local paper blasting a decision of yours or some policy of the school. The media generally cherish such public airings because they are controversial and people like to read information in this form. Some administrators try to answer such letters by responding with a letter to the editor of their own. And so a war of letters develops in the newspaper. The combatants in this exchange tend to lose sight of the fact that the newspaper has little interest in the truth behind the argument. Its main interest is in the news the controversy generates. The issue for those airing their demands in public is one of perception, not one of substance. One former superintendent of schools always tells his administrators: Never wage war with someone who buys ink by the barrel. This is excellent advice when it comes to setting perception.

Most negotiators caught in a public airing of their demands will withdraw until public interest in the case dies down. When they feel that the other party has dropped the public demands, they will move back into negotiations hoping that the pressure will have lessened and the parties can start true negotiations. If forced to make a comment because of the intensity of public pressure, many administrators choose to say that they will not comment on the issues publicly because of the sensitive nature of the negotiations.

Symbols of Power

Are dark blue suits on women and tan raincoats on men symbols of power? What about all the other symbols that our culture associates with power? Do they play a role in setting perception? They certainly do. To ignore this symbolic realm is to deny yourself a powerful way of influencing settlement. The use of these symbols is sometimes referred to as "powerology." A few symbols of power are described here.

Space is an important indicator of power. The more power you think you have, the more space you will put between yourself and others. Conversely, the more equal you feel with others, the less space you will put between yourself and them. This sense of space can be seen when a principal walks into the superintendent's office. If the principal has been called "on the carpet," it means just that. He or she is standing on the carpet while the superintendent is seated behind the desk. The superintendent is communicating power. On the other hand, when the superintendent simply wants to exchange ideas with the principal, the conversation may take place around a coffee table or a conference table where the parties are physically closer. For additional reading on space, see *Body Language and Social Order* by Albert E. Scheflen and Anne Scheflen (Englewood Clifs, NJ: Prentice-Hall, 1972).

Time is another indicator of power. The more unequal the perceived power of the respective parties, the less time is spent in discussion. The more equal the parties perceive themselves to be, the more time is spent in discussion. Time can be a possible limitation on a successful settlement, but it also serves as an indicator of power. Professional people say that "time is money" and talk about "buying time." This language deals with time as a symbol of power. For additional reading see *Body Politics* by Nancy M. Henley (Englewood Cliffs, NJ: Prentice-Hall, 1977).

Dress is also considered a symbol of power, and there have been numerous popular books written on the subject, such as *The New Dress for Success* by John Malloy (New York: Warner Publications, 1988). Dark-colored clothing is considered a symbol of power. Soft colors and pastels have a feeling of gentleness associated with them. Flashes of color, however, such as a red tie or scarf, can augment a dark suit by revealing a person's qualities of daring and drive. Excessive jewelry on women detracts from an image of power because it connotes excess and possessiveness of material things. A few pieces of jewelry, on the other hand, show good taste and a sense of quality. Unbuttoned collars on blouses or shirts are said to reveal that a person is more interested in attention than in the process at hand.

Activity 5-2 deals with these three aspects of power: time, space, and dress.

Before you read the next section, complete activity 5-3.

CHOOSING AN OPTION

The time has come for the participants in the negotiations to claim that piece of the expanded pie they feel is of value to them. Here you will discover whether the perception set you created has worked or whether the other participant has claimed part of your value. The skill of the negotiator here is to reveal an option that provides a

---

ACTIVITY 5-2

To understand the use of symbols of power, consider the last two meetings you had with your boss. After each of the characteristics, write what occurred during your encounter with your boss. To determine how he or she may or may not have used symbols of power to gain influence with you, refer to the text discussion.

1. *Space:* Where did the meeting take place? Where were you located? Where was your boss located?

_____

2. *Time:* Who set the time for the encounter? Did it begin on time? How were distractions handled?

_____

3. *Dress:* Compare how you were dressed with how your boss was dressed.

_____

Now take the same questions and apply them to a situation where you were the boss. How did you use symbols of power to influence one of your staff members?

---

mutually agreeable settlement for all parties but still claims as much value as possible within the zone of agreement. Three different methods to accomplish this goal are described in this section.

Opening Claim

There is general agreement that it is desirable to make the first offer in chosing a settlement option. This is especially true if you know or can intelligently guess the other party's BATNA. Knowing the BATNA enables you to calculate how much value within the zone of agreement you can claim without forcing the other party to walk. Discovering the other's BATNA was discussed earlier, in Chapter Two. It is a piece of information you will need to know. In most school situations you will be able to make an intelligent guess about your opponent's BATNA.

The first offer needs to be strong but not extreme enough to elicit a reciprocal extreme offer from the other party. This opening needs to be seen as a statement of interest or value, not as a demand. Although some people prefer to state their positions as de-

---

ACTIVITY 5-3

As the superintendent, you have proposed that class size be increased by two students per class for the next school year. A member of the school board has asked to meet with you privately to hear why you think this is necessary. What would your opening remark be?

_____

_____

_____

_____

_____

_____

_____

_____

Why did you choose this response? After reading the next section on choosing an option, redo this activity. Compare your opening statement to the type of statement described in this section. How do they differ?

---

mands right from the start in order to communicate a principle, there is generally no long-term advantage to using this opening tactic. The following are some examples of how a demand can be framed to sound like a strong opening statement.

Demand Position

Terry: Helen, stop keeping my students after your class. That makes them late for my class.

Strong Opening Statement

Terry: Helen, I become frustrated when you keep my students late in your class. I can't cover my material with all the students.

Could you possibly try to let your students out as soon as possible after the bell rings?

The difference in the two statements is that in the first Terry makes a demand and stakes out a position. He has no idea or interest in why Helen allows this problem to exist. He will most likely get back an equally extreme position statement from Helen. The result is a conflict, which the building principal will need to resolve.

In the second statement Terry provides Helen with his vested interest. He reveals his feelings and his need to cover the curriculum uniformly. He states his position, but he also opens up the statement to elicit Helen's interest in the situation. Perhaps there is a reason she keeps students late that he needs to know about. In the second example, Terry makes a strong opening statement but provides room for eliciting Helen's interest. Once he has heard from her, he can guess at the zone of agreement within which to negotiate.

In a schematic form, the opening statement would be something like this:

I think _____ because _____ [fact-based rationale], and I would like the following to happen: _____. Do you have a problem with this?

or

I feel _____ because _____ [fact-based rationale], and I would like the following to happen: _____ How do you feel about this?

What happens if you have no idea what the other's BATNA may be, or if you know the other person is irrational and unpredictable? In such cases, let the other party make the first offer. This gives you information about the range of agreement the other person is establishing. Once this information is out, you can counter with your opening statement and establish the range of the settlement.

EXAMPLE

In one famous jury case, the jurors were required to establish a dollar figure to award to a girl as compensation for injuries sustained in a car accident. They were at a loss as to how to determine, out of the infinite possibilities, an exact dollar amount. None of the jurors had any idea of what the others were expecting to give. Some of them feared a prolonged negotiation. They were unsure of what the others' BATNA would be. Uncertain of the others' opening figures, the jurors decided to use a secret ballot on which each juror would write an award figure. They agreed that this would set the range, and the negotiations would then take place within this zone of agreement. The range is outlined in the following figure:

Low Award _____ High Award

$25,000 . . . .$200,000

ZONE OF AGREEMENT

After some discussion and concessions by various jurors, the final decision was that $113,000, or exactly half the difference, would be given as an award.

If this process had not been used, the danger to the jurors was that a prolonged battle could ensue, with the possibility of a deadlock. Consider the scenario if one of the jurors had proposed a million-dollar award. An extreme position would be established by a very strong opening statement. The others would then have two choices. They could use this figure as a focal point and spend the rest of their deliberations negotiating around this figure. Or they could have one or more of the other jurors counter this extreme high demand with an extreme low position, perhaps $10,000. In the first case, the high juror would influence the others through a perceptual set. In the second case, there would be a real chance of prolonged deliberations because the zone of agreement was so wide.

Activity 5-4 gives you some practice in developing strong opening statements.

Here are some strategies you can use to respond to another person's opening statement.

1. *Ignore it.* This is simple. Just pretend you did not hear the statement. Then make your own opening statement. This is a particularly good strategy if you feel you have established a very strong perceptual set. Your statement may overpower the other person's interest statement, which would be silently dropped.

ACTIVITY 5-4

Read each of the following positional statements and change them to strong opening statements using the formula described in the text. Compare your responses to the examples given. Were your responses stronger or weaker than those in the suggested examples? After comparing your answers to the examples, would you rewrite them? How?

1. The library needs to be open longer during the day.

_____

_____

2. The administrators in this district should teach more often so they understand kids.

_____

_____

3. Stop having so many committee meetings!

_____

_____

4. The teachers in this building need to start to coming on time.

_____

_____

SUGGESTED POSITIONAL STATEMENTS

1. I think the library should be open longer during the day because more of the high school students would stay after school to use it. I would suggest leaving the library open for an extra hour. What do you think?

2. I feel the administrators should teach in the classrooms more often because they would be in a position to get to know the students. I would like to propose this to the superintendent. What do you think?

3. I feel we have too many committee meetings because I seem to be attending one at least once a week. I would like to have more task forces developed so the number of formal meetings is reduced. Do you have a problem with this?

4. I really get upset when the teachers in this building come in late. It means I have to cover classes. I would like the teachers' union president to help me in talking to those who come in late at least once a week. What do you think about the union president getting involved in this?

2. *Ask for verification.* After the statement is made, ask the other party to support it with objective data. Once you have received the supporting data, you can center the negotiations around how to interpret this information rather than on the opening statement.

Another way to do this is to ask the party to gain others' support for the proposed option. This is a valuable approach if you feel the person is a maverick with an extreme idea no one would support. Your opponent's failure to gain sufficient support for the idea puts the ball into your court and gives you a chance to provide a strong opening statement.

3. *Link the issues.* In this process you take the other party's statement and link it with a broader issue, which represents your interests as well as the other party's. For example, if the business department in the high school is about to receive a state-of-the art computer, while the technology department is struggling with old equipment, then you might consider the new computer as part of a total school needs package. You agree with the demand from the business department but represent it as a need for the entire school, especially the technology department. In this case, the settlement package would allow the computer to be used by both departments.

Single Text

The use of a single text has been discussed. This is a way of utilizing a perception set as a focal point. The text also can serve as an opening statement. Usually, once a written proposal on a topic has been delivered, the opinions of all participants focus on the document. This technique is particularly useful if there are a large number of people representing different constituencies. It is difficult to get a committee to agree on any one thing through a discussion process. There must be some mechanism to pull together the common feelings and thoughts of the group. A text or proposal written by one or two members of each group provides a central focus for starting negotiations. The assumption is that any item not included in the text cannot be included in the pursuant negotiations.

Skillful negotiators will be sure to include themselves in the group writing the proposal. This is a firm way to bring your interests to the front and ensure that they become part of the negotiation process. It has the same effect as making the opening statement, as discussed before. A good text should contain the following items:

- Purpose of the text
- Proposed action plan (solution)
- Implementation plan
- Outcome (value)

EXAMPLE

An example of the successful use of this technique occurred in a school district where individuals representing the community, the administration, the board of education, and the teaching staff met to determine the achievement needs of the minority students. Although the participants' groups represented a wide range of interests, the discussions that resulted over the next few months sparked a very professional search and review of the educational programs in the district. The task of bringing together all the ideas and discussions to the point of making specific recommendations was enormous. The single text report was adopted as a means of achieving a common statement. A few people on the committee volunteered to write a rough draft of the text and present it to the full twenty-member committee for approval. The final draft report that this committee issued to the public was very similar in essence to the text first issued by the small writing group. When single-text documents are introduced to a group for approval, after having been written by members of the same group, there usually is very little deviation from the draft.

Some school districts use this technique in their negotiations with the teachers' union over the contract. Before the parties sit down to negotiate, each submits a list of interests to the other party. These lists become the basis of all the negotiations. No new interests or new demands are allowed to be added to the list. The advantage of this procedure is that the lists become the focal point of the negotiation, and a single text contract can be hammered out. One disadvantage is that the process loses its flexibility. For example, joint gains may be restricted because linking issues is not possible if no new interests can be brought into the negotiation process.

Taking Hostages

Another technique that is part of skillful negotiations is the ability to listen for, guess at, or conclude from remarks what the other party's prime value may be. This is the one value among all the items discussed that is of the utmost interest to this party, the value he or she wants above all others. Once this value is identified, it can be held hostage.

Some negotiators make the fatal mistake of announcing to their constituents publicly that they will demand above all else that a certain interest be part of the settlement. This is a signal to the other party that this interest can be taken hostage. Once the party has committed him- or herself to this value, it would be very difficult to walk away from the negotiations without securing this interest. That person would suffer a loss of face, a loss of credibility, and possibly even a loss of a leadership position.

The other party now has an opportunity to claim significant gains in this negotiation. As long as the prime value exposed by the first party is within the zone of acceptability, the second party can grant it and still have the opportunity to seize the remainder of the gains. The first party has, in essence, negotiated them away. The following example is a good illustration of the use of this technique.

EXAMPLE

During teachers' union negotiations, the president of the union announced at a rally that he would demand from the superintendent and from the board of education that teachers in the school district who teach special subjects such as art, music, or physical education be given no homeroom assignments. This was his number one demand, he declared for all to hear, amid cheers from the staff. The superintendent immediately realized that this demand could be taken hostage. After consulting with the building-level principals, he realized that with some minor adjustments the few homeroom periods covered by special teachers could be reassigned. In other words, the principals affirmed that this union demand could be within the zone of agreement. Once he had this validation, the superintendent took this demand hostage. The following diagram illustrates the positions:

Union President			Superintendent

A   B   C   D

`. . . . . . . . . . . . . . . . . . . . . .`

ZONE OF AGREEMENT

The superintendent located the union president's demand at point D on the range of options. It was within the zone of agreement, and he could accept it. The union president had miscalculated and had thought his demand would be at point A, at one extreme of the range of possible options. The superintendent now took this demand hostage and told the union president that he would concede on the homeroom issue if the special teachers would be allowed to do a duty assignment in the cafeteria. Previously, special teachers had not been given such duties. The union president tried to negotiate away this demand. But the superintendent came back to the hostage issue and claimed that special teachers would be freed of homeroom duty only if they could be given duties in the lunchroom.

The union president had no other choice. With some minor modifications, the settlement package reflected the demands of both the union president and the superintendent. The superintendent walked away with gains from point B through point D.

The only way to avoid this hostage-taking option is to present your needs as interests rather than as demands. Interests, as discussed earlier in this book, are not position statements and have a wide latitude for interpretation and for satisfaction. It is difficult to take interests hostage because of their flexibility.

HOW TO CLOSE A DEAL

Every teacher knows the value of questioning. Whether it is designed to bring a student back on task, or to test a student's recall, or to lead a student to think deductively, a questioning procedure is a vital skill for the classroom teacher. So too can questioning be used to influence a participant in a negotiation process. The purposes are different, but the skill is the same. The negotiator's purpose may be to elicit a series of small "yeses," which later could add up to a big yes on a proposed settlement, or to excite the other party to a settlement, or to determine what objections stand in the way of the other participant saying yes.

Listed here are a few questioning techniques a skillful negotiator may wish to use to seize an option. These and other questioning skills are elaborated on in *How to Master the Art of Selling.* by Tom Hopkins (New York: Warner Books, 1982).

The Tie-Down

This is a word or phase at the end of a sentence which in fact asks a question. The answer to the question has to be a yes, which implies agreement with the content embedded in the sentence structure. For example, "We're a full team here, aren't we?" The question implies a yes response even though the content of the material may or may not elicit a yes from the respondent. The questioner, by tying down one small "yes," has unconsciously started a positive response set, which may well lead to a full commitment to the settlement option.

Other tie-down words are:

Don't you agree?	Shouldn't we?	Can't you?
Isn't it right?	Don't you agree?	Hasn't she?
Won't you?	Shouldn't we?	Didn't it?

The Softer Tie-Down

This is similar to the tie-down just described, but it is more gentle in its approach. The tie-down word is placed at the beginning of the sentence—for example, "Aren't we a full team here?"

Question-a-Question

This skill requires that you ask a question as a response to every question asked of you. This process allows you to stay in control of the negotiation process and moves the other party closer to saying yes. For example, here the principal is asking one of the department chairs to motivate some of the teachers in the department to run a science fair. The chairperson begins by asking the following question:

Chairperson: Do you mean it is my job to do a science fair?
Principal: Is running a science fair one of your roles?
Chairperson: I never knew it until now.
Principal: Well, does knowing it now make it one of your roles?
Chairperson: Not necessarily?
Principal: What will need to happen for you to allow it to be one of your roles?

Here the principal has moved the reluctant chairperson to start thinking about the science fair. Rather than having the chairperson state a position or say no explicitly, the principal gets the person to think through how to make the science fair become a reality. This is a small step toward a commitment to a yes answer.

Activity 5-5 gives you some practice in getting the other party to make a stronger commitment to a settlement option.

ACTIVITY 5-5

Read each of these questions and change them so that they reflect a stronger commitment to the settlement option from the other party.

1. I wish you were more committed to this agreement.

_____

2. Do you always question whether we handle the discipline efficiently enough?

_____

3. Can you change the way you are going to present this settlement?

_____

TYPICAL ANSWERS

1. Aren't we both in this together?

2. Discipline is handled well in this building, don't you agree?

3. Shouldn't we change the way you are going to present this settlement?

Handling Objections

Often the other participant decides to think things over. When that happens, you are in danger of losing the momentum. What can you do? How can you get back on target and pursue your settlement option? One thing you definitely need to do is not to allow the other person to walk away with an objection to the proposal.

Once the other party leaves the meeting, there are many other doubts that can flesh out the original objection. Without your presence to ward off these doubts, this participant will turn those doubts into a definite no. Here are a few steps to turn the objection around:

1. *Fog the statement.* Whatever the person says, you should agree. You can say that perhaps it is true, or perhaps it needs time to settle in. If the objection is in the form of an attack on you, then respond by giving tacit agreement. You are not conceding that the person is totally right, just partially. By your response you are taking the attack quality out of the other's statement. That is why this technique is called fogging the statement. The other party does not know where to go. He or she does not know how to pursue the objection. Here is an example:

Principal: Well, perhaps you are right. I gave a hasty proposal here.

or

Principal: Yes, sometimes I do favor the English department.

2. *Make an absurd objection.* Here you are doing two things. First, you are keeping the other party engaged by talking. He or she has not moved out the door yet. Second, you are fishing for your opponent's objection to your proposal. By offering an absurd objection, one you make up on the spot, you hope to ferret out the truth. This information is vital to you to counter the other person's internal doubts. For example, in this case the principal has just told the superintendent that he needs to think over the proposal:

Superintendent: It must be that you think I don't like you?
Principal: No, no. It's not that at all. What gave you such an idea? It is just that . . . that I'm not sure the teachers will go for it.

Here the superintendent has elicited the principal's true objection. He can now proceed to deal with a real objection.

3. *Help with the objection.* Once the objection has been made you will no doubt have the other party stating one of his or her real values. In the case described here, the teacher involvement was a real interest or value to the principal even before accepting the superintendent's proposal. This is a powerful value to this principal. If the superintendent wants the principal to adopt his proposal, he can do one of two things. The first is that he can order him to do it:

Superintendent: The teachers are not an issue here. I want you to do it.

The second is that he can help him clarify the issues with the teachers and provide whatever support is needed at that end to meet the principal's needs.

Superintendent: Tell me more about what you expect the teachers to think about this. Maybe I can help you in delivering this proposal. There are things I can do to help you.

What Happens When You Do Not Like the Offer?

What happens when it is the other party who is trying to tie you down to an agreement that you cannot accept? In such cases you need to say no. It is appropriate to say no to certain kinds of agreements. It saves time, presents you as being honest, presents your values again, and in the long run makes you feel good about the process.

You should say no when one or more of the following are true:

- You are being committed to an action that you feel is morally wrong.
- You are tired.
- It is the first offer.
- The offer is presented as a threat.
- It is presented as "take it or leave it."
- You are being asked to commit others before you have consulted with them.
- You feel the other party is not regarding you with respect or treating your interests as sincere.
- After an agreement has been made, the other party asks for more (referred to in selling as "side conditions").

CLOSING

At this stage, you need to tie down the parties to the agreement and formalize the settlement. If the two skills described earlier in the discussion of this tactic—shaping a perception and choosing a settlement option—have been successful, you should have few problems bringing the negotiation process to a successful conclusion.

Simply put, if you feel the time is right to make an agreement, you need to ask for it. Assuming your opening statement was strong and well received and assuming the final discussions are centering around minor issues with respect to your option, you should take the step and leap toward an agreement. At times this step involves making minor concessions and then asking, in one way or another, "Can we reach a settlement on this issue?" A yes will require you to formalize the agreement. A no or a maybe will require that you return to Tactic 3 and start exerting leverage to settle.

Forms of Agreement

This agreement process can take three forms.

Agreement on Principle

This happens when the bargaining range is still very large. The parties can agree only on the procedures of continued negotiation, not on the content.

With some conflicts, the best alternative to a negotiated agreement (BATNA) is to keep talking rather than just walk away. Walking away could very well escalate the conflict, and that is an alternative that neither party can endorse.

The value of an agreement on procedures should not be minimized. It is a formal agreement, one that is absolutely necessary if continued progress is to be made. This form of agreement may occur in a school when the principal meets with a very angry parent before school begins and needs time during the day to gather facts and talk to all the interested parties before a decision can be made. The parent may have to hurry off to work without waiting for an immediate response to her particular demand. This interlude in time is part of an agreement to agree on the procedures that the principal will need to follow before a resolution can be formulated.

Oral Agreement

A second type of formal agreement is an oral one. This is the most common type among school personnel. It is an excellent form of agreement between parties who know and work with each other every day. There is no need to have a written agreement because everyone's word of honor is sufficient to formalize the process. In some cases a formal written agreement might even be construed as insulting.

Often, when a dispute has been public and an agreement is reached, it is common for the disputants to show some gesture of friendliness. Such a demonstration involves personal risk, but it also supports and affirms the settlement. In one district the superintendent of schools attended a surprise birthday party for the union president given at the school building where she worked. This risky gesture affirmed to the school staff that the agreement just negotiated was solid because it was built on the personal relationship between the two.

Written Agreement

The third form of agreement is the written, formal one, detailing at length who will do what over a certain period of time to implement the stages of the settlement package. In labor negotiations the written agreement takes the form of a contract. Few school disputes are resolved with such formally worded written statements. Having a written summary, however, is very wise if the agreement involves many different people in a school district or building. Often people forget parts of the agreement or forget that they are responsible for some of the implementation, or have a different analysis of the solution once it is being implemented. If one or more of the parties needed to implement the settlement were not present at the negotiations, those parties not only need to have the resolution process summarized for them but also need to have a written summary of the settlement stages.

Congratulate Yourself

The final resolution is the one that takes place in your mind. Conflict resolution is a stressful process. Some thrive on it, and others run from it. For a school administrator, managing conflict is a life-long professional obligation. Because it is part of the profession, you need to feel good about getting involved in these resolution processes. To do this, you need to take time to review mentally what happened during a conflict, what feelings were generated, and how the settlement was finally reached. There may be times when you wonder if you did, in fact, manage to resolve the conflict. You may have second thoughts or doubts about some of the things you did or said. You may even consider the process a failure. The essential point, however, is that you realize that you tried to manage the conflict with all your wisdom, truth, and integrity. The settlement outcome you helped form attempted to undo a conflict that was causing people stress and consuming large amounts of professional time and energy. Because of your efforts, the school is a better place. You had the courage and the knowledge at least to try to undo the pain, anger, or injustice that prevailed.

SUMMARY

The final settlement process involves finding an agreement that satisfies your interests. Getting the best possible settlement or the most gains from the various possible settlement options depends on such skills as setting expectations, using focal points, setting limits, using concessions, communication, using symbols of power, and using language. Although both parties will gain something from the resolution process, it is possible that one party will seize more of the mutual gains than the other. The process of getting an advantageous settlement creates the tension and excitement of committing yourself to an option.

Three methods of moving the other party to accept the option you want were discussed. Methods of closing the deal and handling objections were described. In preparing the settlement for final approval, the reader was instructed in how to formulate the formal settlement using a principled oral or written agreement procedure.

MICHAEL'S CONFLICT

Having agreed to settle the conflict, the principal was ready to commit the parties to a settlement option. First he decided to set the perception in such a way that it reflected the conflicting values with respect to time. This move significantly strengthened his bargaining hand.

He decided to use a focal point. He took Michael's report card and pointed out to the parents that even though Michael had received an F for the first quarter, there were three more school quarters left to grade as well as a slot to record the final average for the year. He emphasized that the final grade was the most important, as it reflected all the work of the student and was the only grade viewed by the high school teachers. In other words, Michael had four more English grades to receive, and the last of these was the most significant.

The report card, specifically the empty grade-recording slots, served as the focal point. This was concrete and specific, and it dealt with the issues concerning time. It also pointed out vividly to the parents the importance of Michael's future acquisition of knowledge.

In committing to an option, the principal proposed the first settlement. As you will recall, he knew the parents' BATNA: to write a letter to the board of education or to see the superintendent of schools. He also guessed that he had time before the parents used this BATNA. Knowing this, he decided to come out with a strong opening offer. To reinforce this offer, he took as hostage one of the parents' prime demands, that their son be removed from Mr. Fritz's class. As you know, Mr. Fritz had told the principal that he did not want Michael in his class after the parents had rejected his first concession. The principal, however, withheld this information from the parents. He still had the authority to transfer a student, and he kept this as one of his options.

In taking a hostage, the principal informed the parents this way:

Principal: Mr. and Mrs. James, I think I have a way we can reach an agreement on this problem. I can transfer Michael from Mr. Fritz's class, but I will need to make arrangements on his grading for the remainder of the school term. We usually do not move students like this. I will need to ask some leeway [*translation:* concessions] from you on the grading.

The parents, realizing that their prime value was to get Michael out of that class, were ready for any option.

Mrs. James: Why, sure, we will help. I understand this is unusual. We would surely like to cooperate with you. What is your idea?

The principal then stated the settlement agreement.

Principal: To begin, the first quarter grade, the F, has to stay. The reason for this is that I cannot undo unilaterally a grading system in this school. However, I understand your concerns about whether Michael deserves this grade. What is more important to me and, I am sure, to you is that Michael learn the curriculum. So, to make sure that this happens, I will transfer him to another teacher. This teacher will be responsible for Michael's grades for the rest of the year. She will fill in these empty grading slots. [Here he points out the slots on the report card.] Now, about that F. I will ask the new teacher, when she averages for the fifth and final grade in June, to exclude the F. Since the new teacher teaches the curriculum in a different sequence, Michael will be required to relearn some of the first-quarter work, and he will be required to catch up to where his class-mates are.

Mr. James: That sounds very good to me. As long as the boy is out of Fritz's class, I'm happy.

Mrs. James: It's a good idea. But how will we know if the new teacher will allow this?

The parents are now asking for a formal agreement. The principal responded using a warm tie-down:

Principal: Isn't it great that we agree on this!

The parents nod agreement. The principal now uses an oral agreement followed up with a written summary.

Principal: I understand your concerns. Let's start by saying this will start tomorrow. I will inform Mr. Fritz and the new teacher of the change. I will ask the guidance counselor to meet with Michael to explain what happened and to tell him that the ball is in his court. He now needs to work and prove he has the ability.

He then addresses the internal communications concern.

Principal: I will speak personally with Michael's new teacher and explain this new arrangement. I suspect she will agree to it if Michael agrees to do the extra work. A deal is a deal here. Nothing comes free. [*Translation:* I attached conditions on your prime value after taking it hostage.] So that everyone knows what's what, I will draft a summary letter of this agreement and mail it out to all parties. Any questions?

At this point Mr. James tries to attach a side issue to the settlement.

Mr. James: You know, I have problems with the social studies material also. Can we talk about this?

The principal says no:

Principal: One issue at a time. I do not think we should discuss Michael's case any further today. We've covered a lot of territory.

As the parents agree and head for the door, the counselor affirms and locks in the agreement by saying to the parents:

Counselor: I hope you realize what has happened here. He [the principal] does not do this kind of thing every day. He made a lot of concessions to help everyone. You got a very good deal.

References

Carew, Jack. (1987). *You'll Never Get No for an Answer.* New York: Simon and Schuster.

Hewitt, J. P., & Stokes, R. (1975). "Disclaimers." *American Sociological Review, 40,* 1–11.

Leritz, Len. (1987). *No-Fault Negotiating.* Portland, OR: Pacifica Press.

Malley, John T. (1988). *The New Dress for Success.* New York: Warner Publications.

Mehrabian, A. (1972). *Nonverbal Communication.* Chicago: Aldine-Atherton.

Raiffa, Howard. (1985). "Post Settlement Settlements." *Negotiation Journal, 1,* 9–12.

Scheflen, A. E., & Scheflen, A. (1972). *Body Language and Social Order.* Englewood Cliffs, NJ: Prentice-Hall.

Schellin, Thomas C. (1960). *The Strategy of Conflict.* Cambridge, MA: Harvard University Press.

CONFLICT RESOLUTION GUIDE

Each chapter in this book contains a Conflict Resolution Guide. You can use this guide as a worksheet for any ongoing conflict resolutions in which you are involved. It can serve as a checklist for determining where you are in the resolution process and where you need to go.

1. *Getting what you want:* Here it is advisable to prepare a diagram on the zone of agreement, as discussed in this chapter. This will give you a visual representation of the various options. To help you, a blank has been prepared.

Other's   Your
Demand _____ _____/ _____Demand
                              ZONE OF AGREEMENT

2. *Influencing others:* Listed here are a number of strategies. Pick three and detail how you would carry them out.

   Expectation _____

   Focal point _____

   Limitations _____

   Concessions _____

   Communication _____

   Symbols of power _____

   Language _____

3. *Getting the other to commit to an option:* Choose one or more to help you in this process.

   Opening claim statement _____

   _____

   _____

   Single text_____

   _____

Taking a hostage (any prime values to which the other is committed)

_____

_____

_____

_____

_____

4. *Methods to close:* Choose one or more and write out your tie-down.

_____

_____

_____

_____

5. *Objections:* Do you anticipate any objections?

_____

_____

_____

6. *Choosing a form to close on:* Will it be an agreement on principle, an oral agreement, a written agreement, or a combination of all three?

_____

_____

_____

_____

7. *Conclusion:* Do not forget to congratulate yourself!

Conflicting interests and common interests need to be explored so that different options can be discovered or created by the participants. Six methods for devising settlement options were described.

1. Are there conflicting interests? List values and nonvalues for each of the participants.

Conflict of interest_____

_____

_____

Conflict of risk_____

_____

_____

Conflict of forecast, time, resources, and so on_____

_____

_____

2. Are there common interests? List the values and nonvalues for each of the participants.

_____

_____

_____

_____

3. Can the values and nonvalues listed here be blended to generate a number of settlement options? Choose one or more of the techniques listed here to generate options.

Brainstorming ideas_____

_____

_____

_____

Discussion group ideas_____

_____

_____

_____

_____

Mediation_____

_____

_____

_____

Role playing_____

_____

_____

_____

Outside resources_____

_____

_____

_____

Arbitration_____

_____

_____

CHAPTER SIX

Lies, Deceit, and Games

Up to this point we have considered how to use a developer model of negotiation to resolve conflicts. What happens when you encounter someone who is not interested in seeking joint gains or developing a resolution that satisfies mutual interests? What should you do if the other party wants to negotiate a resolution that ignores your interests and satisfies only his or her own interest? How do you counter the various tactics that party might employ against you?

There is no one clear or consistent way to deal with the distasteful or unethical side of negotiations without getting fully involved. If the other party is determined to force you to give up your demands or your interests in the situation, he or she will try all sorts of tactics to move you off your position. Sometimes the other party will test you to determine how committed you are. At other times your opponent will exert considerable pressure over a long period of time to wear you down. You will have to be prepared to deal with these tactics and the pressure that is brought to bear on you.

This chapter illustrates how to deal with those who use lies, deceit, or various tactical games to influence your decision-making powers during negotiation. You will learn some specific tactics to counter these games and ways to develop your own powerful personal resources to counter any possible unethical behavior that may arise.

Before you look at others, however, Activity 6-1 ("How Machiavellian Are You?") will allow you to look at how you use deceit to influence others. Take a minute or two to complete the questions.

What is a machiavellian? Named after a sixteenth-century court figure of Florence, Niccolo di Bernardo Machiavelli, a machiavellian is known for the use of guile and deceit to influence and control others. A person scoring high on this scale (a high machiavellian) would be prone to use the lies, deceit, and games described in this chapter to gain concessions at the bargaining table. He or she would use people to seek personal gain, and would be more concerned with ends than with means. A low machiavellian would not use such tactics but would be more influenced by the opinion of others and the effect a decision would have on another person. Low machiavellians bow to social pressure and are heavily influenced in face-to-face encounters. Those who score in the average range tend to have a blend of the two traits. Those scoring toward the low average end favor low machiavellian behaviors but would not rule out the occasional use of the tactics of a high machiavellian. The opposite would hold true for those who scored in the high average range. They would be prone to use high machiavellian tactics but would not rule out the behavior of a low machiavellian. For further information on machiavellianism, see *Studies in Machiavellianism* by Richard Christie and Florence L. Geis (New York: Academic Press, 1970).

WHO LIES?

The answer to this question is simple. Everyone lies. According to recent research, adults admit to lying, on average, thirteen times a week, or a little less than twice a day. See "Lies Can Point to Mental Disorders or Signal Normal Growth" by Daniel Goleman, *New York Times,* May 17, 1988, p. C1. Lying is so common that most mental health practitioners see lying as part of normal growth and development because it is part of social life. In fact, a child's first lie, between the ages of two and four, is seen as a necessary step in normal cognitive development.

In determining the reason behind the lie, it is important to keep in mind that lies vary in the amount of guilt and stress in-

ACTIVITY 6-1

HOW MACHIAVELLIAN ARE YOU?

Directions: After each of the following questions, circle the correct number response that best represents your attitude.

1. The best way to handle people is to tell them what they want to hear.

Disagree		Neutral	Agree	
A Lot	A Little		A Little	A lot
1	2	3	4	5

2. When you ask someone to do something for you, it is best to give the real reasons for wanting it rather than give reasons that might carry more weight.

Disagree		Neutral	Agree	
A Lot	A Little		A Little	A Lot
1	2	3	4	5

3. Anyone who completely trusts anyone else is asking for trouble.

Disagree		Neutral	Agree	
A Lot	A Little		A Little	A Lot
1	2	3	4	5

4. It is hard to get ahead without cutting corners here and there.

Disagree		Neutral	Agree	
A Lot	A Little		A Little	A Lot
1	2	3	4	5

5. It is safest to assume that all people have a vicious streak and it will come out when they are given a chance.

Disagree		Neutral	Agree	
A Lot	A Little		A Little	A Lot
1	2	3	4	5

6. One should take action only when sure it is morally right.

Disagree		Neutral	Agree	
A Lot	A Little		A Little	A Lot
1	2	3	4	5

7. Most people are basically good and kind.

Disagree		Neutral	Agree	
A Lot	A Little		A Little	A Lot
1	2	3	4	5

8. There is no excuse for lying to someone else.

Disagree		Neutral	Agree	
A Lot	A Little		A Little	A Lot
1	2	3	4	5

9. Most men forget more easily the death of their father than the loss of their property.

Disagree		Neutral	Agree	
A Lot	A Little		A Little	A Lot
1	2	3	4	5

10. Generally speaking, men won't work hard unless they are forced to do so.

Disagree		Neutral	Agree	
A Lot	A Little		A Little	A Lot
1	2	3	4	5

volved, the consequences, and whether they were planned or not. Perhaps an understanding of the reasons people lie can best be found in the type of lies they use.

   1. *White Lies:* These are lies that are used to smooth over social situations. They are the most common type of lies and are of

---

———— SCORING ————

To find your score, place the numbers you have checked on the following questions on the line provided and then add them.

    1. ___ **2.** ___ **3.** ___ **4.** ___ **5.** ___ **9.** ___ **10.** ___ **Total**___

For the other questions, reverse the numbers you have checked (5 becomes 1, 4 is 2, 2 is 4, and 1 is 5) Place these new numbers for the remaining questions on the line provided and add them.

    6. ___   **7.** ___   **8.** ___   **Total**_____

Now add your two subtotals together. Record this score in the box provided here.

INTERPRETATION

On a random sample of American adults, the average score was 25 (Christie & Geis, 1970). Your score can be interpreted as follows:

10 to 16: Low machiavellian

17 to 36: Average machiavellian

37 to 50: High machiavellian

---

mutual benefit. For example, in these excerpts the administrator is lying to help the conversation move along:

> *Of course I remember the science exhibit you did last year.*

> *I love being superintendent in this city. It is so interesting.*

    2. *Helping lies:* These lies primarily serve to help another person. During a recent student government election one of the defeated candidates asked the principal how close the election was. In fact, the student had lost by a landslide. Rather than make the student feel even more rejected, the principal simply said that the election was a close one. This type of lie is used very often. In these excerpts the administrator is lying to help the other person.

No, I do not know if you have been selected for the gifted program. [Here he is waiting to allow the counselor to reveal this information.]

I do not know where the staff cuts will come this year. [Here she is waiting until an alternative plan she has proposed to the superintendent is discussed.[

3. *Pathological lies:* These are the type of lies produced by people with mental problems or dysfunctions. They are usually out of touch with reality, and their lies are unrelated to the facts. An example would be the administrator who had a paranoid belief that certain students were out to destroy his car. This administrator hired a private detective to watch his car while it was parked in the school parking lot. Unfortunately, local police on a routine patrol found this detective outside the school and questioned his activities. When the police approached the school administrator to verify the detective's story, the administrator lied and claimed he knew nothing of it.

4. *Self-Beneficial lies:* These are the type of lies that hurts most of us. It is the lie that someone else uses for personal gain. This type of lie fosters the loser–winner competition. The goal is to make you the loser by distorting the truth. The lie becomes a means to an end. We have all been victims of such a lie. Here are some examples:

I speak for the superintendent when I ask you to change this.

I remember looking at this before. The amount we spent last year was double.

CAN LIES BE DETECTED?

In negotiations, there is always some tension between how much to trust the other person and reveal your interests and positions and how much to mistrust and hold back. This is a lot like playing a game of cards. How much can you safely show to remain in the game without revealing the winning card until the end? This tension is the dilemma of conflict resolution. You cannot trust the other completely or you will be "taken to the cleaners." Yet without some trust, no negotiation can take place.

It is best to negotiate over the interests and agendas involved, not the people. Keep the personalities removed from the bargaining considerations, and you will have little difficulty in dealing with issues of trust versus mistrust. This common middle ground allows you to bargain while maintaining your integrity and, in the process, to discover with the other person the range of agreement over which the conflict can be resolved. A common rule of thumb is to suspend judgment until you have the facts. Trust the facts, not the other person. Discover the facts, share the information, verify them for yourself, and use them as the basis of building an agreement.

In the short term, lying works. Those who lie use the falsification of information to their own advantage. They distort information in such a manner that their interests in the conflict seem to be different from what they really are. In the process, they hope to maximize their own gain at the direct expense of your interests in the conflict. For a detailed analysis of the use of lying in negotiations, see "Lying and Deception" by Roy J. Lewicki, in *Negotiating in Organizations,* edited by Max H. Bazerman (Beverly Hills, CA: Sage Publications, 1983).

In the long term, however, lies are usually discovered. If there is any ongoing relationship of the parties involved, this discovery will destroy the liar's future bargaining power and severely damage the relationship on which the bargaining is built.

Can lying be detected? The answer is yes. Most people can detect, even unconsciously, if someone is lying. Liars have a problem of congruence. They need to bring together their external self (voice, nonverbal behavior, tone) and their internal self (feelings, attitudes, values). This takes enormous energy because there is a difference between the two.

A liar is trying to pretend. Only the most pathological can pull it off successfully all the time. The discrepancy between the external and the internal self can be detected by most people. In fact, most liars give themselves away by their body movements, voice pitch, or facial expressions. Specifically, liars mask their smiles more often than not. Smiling lips and muscular activity around the eyes can be detected on the faces of truth-tellers. On liars, movement of the upper lip and lip corners, indicating disgust, fear, contempt, or sadness, can often be observed. Because it is beyond the scope of this book to teach you to detect a liar, you are referred for more information to Paul Ekman, Wallace Friesen, and Maureen O'Sullivan's article "Smiles When Lying," in the *Journal of Personality and Social Psychology,* Vol. 54, March 1988, pp. 414–420.

WHAT TO DO ABOUT A LIAR

You have three choices when you discover a liar. Your choice is based on your overall strategy for trying to settle the conflict. On the one hand, you need to preserve the other's pride or help save face. On the other hand, you need to remove the false information from the bargaining table.

1. *Ignore it.* You can ignore a lie if you feel that the facts are not important to the overall case. If you become involved in a discussion about the lie, it may distort your argument. If the falsification is not crucial to the case, simply ignore the lie and the erroneous information. Perhaps if you ignore the lies, the other person will do the same. In any case, keep your guard up and be aware of future attempts at deception.

An example of this may occur during a meeting with an angry parent. This mother's child is being suspended from school for fighting. The mother is protesting the suspension, stating that her child is a good student and has never been in trouble with the principal before. The principal knows the child has been sent to the school's time-out room at least three times by different teachers, and knows that the parent is aware of this. Yet the principal ignores the lie in favor of concentrating on the behavior that occurred during this fight. He judges that if he gets into an argument with the mother about how many times the child has been in the time-out room, he will lose his focus on the present problem.

2. *Acknowledge it.* In these cases you have decided that the falsification is serious enough to warrant your intervention to save your interests. You decide, however, to allow the other person to save face. Your tactic is to have the other party simply disengage from the lie. Most people, when caught in a lie, try to rationalize their way out of it. Rationalization is a defense mechanism whereby one substitutes a "good" reason for a bad one. In this process they try to convince not only you but even themselves that no lie was intended.

For example, after finding out that a furniture order did not go out on a bid as required by district policies, the superintendent asks the business manager why this happened. The manager responds:

> *Well, I did specify that all the furniture orders go out on bid. I thought that this order, however, was different because of the items. Besides, I thought we could save money.*

The advantage of acknowledging a lie is that it puts the other person on notice that you are aware of the attempt and that he or she has been caught. The other advantage is that it allows the other to save face gracefully. You may need this other party to have his or her pride intact if there is ever going to be a successful resolution of the conflict.

3. *Confront it.* Sometimes you need to confront the other person directly with the lie. You need to have the falsification totally removed from the table in such a manner that the other party is challenged to become an equal partner in the bargaining process. When used correctly, a confrontation can invoke the other person to start looking at the negotiation as a venture to develop *mutual gains.*

Confrontation should never be an attack on the other person. Although it will most likely make your opponent uncomfortable and perhaps cause him or her to lose face, it should not destroy or be punitive. We have all been in conversations, however, where the confrontation has turned into an attack. The outcome of such behavior is that the other person either goes on the defensive or simply removes him- or herself from the conversation. The end result is that the conflict remains unresolved. The two examples that follow illustrate this point. The first is an attack confrontation:

> *John, you told me you talked with the teachers. This is a lie. You spoke with one or two. Why did you lie to me?*

In this example, John is put on the defensive immediately. His response will certainly be an explanation of why he talked to only a few teachers. The real issue of what he learned is temporarily forgotten.

The second example is one of an unmasking confrontation:

> *John, when you told me you had spoken with the teachers, I assumed that you had spoken with all of them. I did not realize that you meant only one or two. Perhaps I was unclear*

here or you were not assertive enough. In any case, now that
this has been brought to my attention, I suggest that you go
try again and see if all the teachers can be contacted.

In this example John has lost some face, and his distortion has
been unmasked. However, John has been challenged to go out and
do the task correctly. The superintendent now can get the information he wants and can move toward resolving the conflict.

Activity 6-2 gives you some practice in using confrontation
skillfully, and Table 6-1 offers some tips for confrontation.

HANDLING DECEPTION

Deception, as defined here, is different from lying. In lying, the person presents false information. In deception, the person tries to
conceal or misrepresent the truth. Although both strategies are
dishonest and have the same goal, they are very different when implemented. Deception takes more work, is harder to accomplish,
requires more cleverness, and is harder to detect.

Deception involves distorting the information flow in such a
manner that others begin to doubt the veracity of their own information or their own value system. A deceiver uses manipulation,
and what is manipulated is your imagination, your feelings, your
needs, and your knowledge. How each of these is manipulated will
be described next.

Your Imagination

We all have our own fantasy world. Some of it is shared, but most of
it is private. Some of it is enjoyable, some of it is neutral, and some
of it is scary. A clever deceiver will probe your fantasy world in
order to exploit it. For example, the car salesperson will try to determine how you envision yourself in your fantasy world and then
try to get you to buy a car or extra options for a car in order to fulfill
this fantasy. In the following example, a parent touches on a new
principal's private fears that perhaps he is in over his head in trying to run a school.

Now, you can't tell me that you know everything about this
school. I know more than you do. Three of my kids went
through here. Trust me, I want you to succeed here. I will let

```
┌─────────────────────────────────────────────────────────────────────┐
```

━━ ACTIVITY 6-2 ━━

As a building principal, you have discussed at a meeting of department chairs the need to take a textbook inventory in order to determine budget planning for the next school year. The math department chair has submitted a count of math textbooks that is well below what you know to exist in the school. You suspect that this chairperson has deliberately set a low total figure so that the math department will have a budget increase greater than the other departments receive. You need to decide how to deal with this suspected lie.

Listed here are a number of possible outcomes or goals you wish to achieve as a result of confronting this chairperson. Check those goals you wish to achieve. The category with the largest number of checkmarks will determine the tactic to use.

If you wish to

_____ save face for the other party,

_____ not remove falsification from the discussions,

then *ignore* the lie.

If you wish to

_____ save face for the other party,

_____ possibly but not definitely remove falsification from the discussions,

then *acknowledge* the lie.

If you wish to

_____ not save face for the chairperson,

_____ definitely remove the falsification from the discussions,

then *confront* the lie.

Which tactic did you choose and why? Explain your answer.

_____

_____

_____

If you were the assistant superintendent and not the building principal, would your choice of tactic have been different? Why or why not? Please explain your answer.

_____

_____

_____

TABLE 6-1. Confrontation Tips

Never confront values or feelings, only behavior:
"I think you messed this one up."
not
"I think your judgment leaves a lot to be desired."
Confront with empathy:
"I understand how you thought this could be."
not
"I do not give a damn about what you thought."
Confront with less dogmatism and more suggestiveness:
"Perhaps you did not go far enough here."
not
"You did not care to do the whole job".
Confront to maintain the relationship:
"MaryJo, I need to work with you on this, but . . ."
not
"Well, this about destroys our working together."
Confront in small steps:
"The issue of teacher coverage begins with first period."
not
"The issue of teacher coverage is a huge problem."

you in on the true goings on, including how to handle that superintendent of yours.

Here the parent is probing the new principal's possible fears that the position may be overwhelming.

Your Feelings

We all have a value system that tells us what is right or wrong. We all have a sense of mission: where we want our school or our district to go. Your sense of value and of mission is uniquely yours. You communicate your values to others daily in how you act, what you say, and what you give your attention to. A deceiver will try to understand your value system perfectly, perhaps better than you yourself do, and then try to exploit it. The negative feelings that are manipulated are commonly those of guilt, anxiety, and shame. Your pride is the positive feeling most often manipulated. In the following remark, the assistant tries to manipulate the principal by fostering guilt about an evaluation.

> *Now, Bob, won't you feel a little guilty giving a good evalua-*
> *tion to that teacher? That teacher has had a terrible year.*
> *Then how will you be able to face yourself when you also*
> *give a good evaluation to someone else, who really de-*
> *serves one.*

Your Knowledge

This is quite common. Here the deceiver tells you everything he or
she knows, but implies that he or she knows a great deal more.
This is an information bluff. In so doing the deceiver is hoping to
draw you out and have you fill in the missing information. For example, you may refer to a written document on the subject matter.
The deceiver perceives this document as being crucial to the talks.
When you ask him if he has read it, he says that he has but that he
cannot quite recall the specifics of what you are referring to. He
asks you to brief him.

Your Needs

We all have needs. These needs were discussed in Chapter Two
under the tactics of determining your agenda in the resolution
meeting. One of our primary needs is for social approval. Nobody
wants to be left out, made a fool of, or ignored. A deceiver will go out
of his or her way to be friendly with you. He or she may take you to
lunch, give you a friendly call once in a while, or come to your side
with words of support when the going gets rough. Yet the deceiver's
friendliness has a hidden barb. Eventually he or she will try to exploit this relationship to gain something that is not morally right.
In manipulating your need for social approval, there is an attempt
to make you feel either that you owe or that you are about to lose a
friend. Here is an example from one of the PTA officers:

> *Joe, I don't ask for much. I'm always there if you need some-*
> *thing. Well, now I'm asking a favor. I will be eternally grate-*
> *ful. Could you place my son in the advanced science class?*
> *It would only be between us. You know he can do it. I would*
> *not be asking if he could not do it. He can. You know that. I*
> *know you can do this. I would be very appreciative.*

Deceivers are hard to catch with the goods. The very act of deception is surrounded with layers of protection for the deceiver. A good deceiver will try to get you to think that the deception is in fact something you believed in all along. Often you can discover a deception if you listen to your own feelings about the encounter. If you feel a sense of awkwardness or confusion, then you need to stop the action and evaluate what is going on in the relationship. Listening to your feelings in this way will signal you that you need to look for the deception.

Your best protection against deception is your own well-developed ethical belief system. If you know what you stand for and believe in what you are doing, it will be hard to manipulate you. On the other hand, if you are unsure of what is important to you, have no developed personal mission statement, and have yet to project your value system into your day-to-day operations, then you will be vulnerable to deception. If you are interested in working on your personal mission statement, the section at the end of this chapter will be of help.

Other measures to defend against deception are the use of the confrontation tactics already discussed. These are as valid for dealing with a deceiver as they are for dealing with a liar. In addition, Table 6-2 offers tips on how to deal with deceivers you feel possess high machiavellian qualities. As you may recall, such people use all types of tactics to deceive and manipulate.

UNDOING PHONY NEGOTIATION

Phony negotiation happens when the other party agrees to resolve a conflict but refuses to discuss meaningful issues and interests at the bargaining table. Your opponent may stall or start to move the talks onto less important issues. Sometimes the other party will stall negotiations as a way of waiting for the context to change before deciding to settle the issues. As you may know, the Korean War "peace" talks went on for a long time before a cease-fire was established. The North Koreans were under pressure to talk but were hoping for a major improvement on the battlefield before the real issues had to be settled.

Use the following procedures to move a phony negotiation to a purposeful negotiation.

TABLE 6.2. Tips to Unmask Deception

---

1. *Getting caught:* High machiavellians are not upset at getting caught in deception. They see deception as a tactic, not as part of a relationship, so getting caught is seen as one of the necessary risks of the game. Sometimes they expect to be caught, but usually they expect to get away with the deception. Do not expect a large emotional reaction to your unmasking attempts. High machiavellians rarely display emotions of guilt or remorse.

2. *Changing through influence:* Deceivers respond effectively to outside influence. They are attracted to people with high prestige. They respect authority and will respond to the directions offered by people they see as either attractive or as possessing power. If, as a school administrator, you are in a situation where you feel you possess neither, you will need to bring someone else into the bargaining discussions. This additional person may be present for only a brief time, but it will be enough to let the other party know you have that outside person's support.

3. *Changing through incentive:* Deceivers will not change simply because what you tell them contradicts their perception. They will not be influenced to look at how your facts or information can be applied to their view. What will influence them, however, are incentives, hard logic, threats and rewards. You can manipulate deceivers if you can apply one of these three influences.

4. *Changing the ambiguity:* Deceivers thrive on ambiguity. If directions are not clear, supervision is lacking, or accountability is scant, deceivers will exploit the situation to meet their interests. They are the ones who will ask questions to determine the limits of the zone of acceptability. If you suspect that manipulation is going on, you may need to tighten up the ground rules.

In the following example, the principal is trying to help a math teacher improve the student passing rate.

> *Now Elizabeth, I will need to look at your lesson plan book every week. I would like to see goals and samples of the weekly worksheets you have developed.*

5. *Changing the resistance:* Deceivers will resist your efforts to change through influence, incentive, and structure. They will look you in the eye and lie. In fact, good deceivers lie more plausibly than the average person. They confess to their deception less often and will put up enormous resistance to your attempts to change them. They will change, however, when they feel that you are stubborn, persistent, and consistent. If you come on strong enough to them about changing, they will eventually respond positively.

---

1. *Ask what the purpose of the meeting may be.* You need to set expectations right off. Let the other parties tell you why they are there. At least they are affirming their goals in public. You may need to help them with this, as they may not even know why they are negotiating.

2. *Listen to their objections.* Whatever their objections, you need to listen to the other parties. In fact, ask them to elaborate. This will give you a true sense of the problem and of how firm they are about stalling. If they go on at length in their elaboration, you can safely guess that they are into the stalling phase of the negotiation.

3. *Do not argue with them.* Whatever you do, avoid the pitfall of arguing with the other parties over their objections. Such arguments are useless because they will not move the negotiation off square one nor will they convince the other parties of the fruitlessness of their objections.

4. *Answer each objection.* In answering each objection, calmly stick to the facts and the information you have. Rephrase the other parties' objections one by one and then address them one by one. Compare and contrast the strengths and weaknesses of your own viewpoint and interests with those of what you perceive to be the other party's interests. Try to keep the focus on the interests of the parties. It is too early in the negotiation process to try to convince the other parties to reach a settlement. They do not want to hear that yet. The focus, again, should be on helping the other parties clarify their interests in the conflict.

5. *Affirm the interest.* Keep mentioning the interests involved in the conflict. This can be done in the form of questions, statements, or declarations. Here are some examples:

Question: "We have identified your interest in this conflict, haven't we?"
Statement: "I'm glad that we see the interests involved in this conflict. They are . . ."
Declaration: "I am announcing to all involved that the interests involved in this conflict are . . ."

6. *Move on.* At this point, move the negotiation on to the next phase. This involves a simple but strong statement to the effect that you are now ready to move the whole conflict to the next phase—developing options to settle. Go back to earlier sections of this book to read about steps for achieving this.

GAMES THEY PLAY

In every bargaining process a number of psychological games are played. They are used to manipulate the process in favor of one party. Although some of the games are consciously employed by the other side, there are also some games that are used against you of which even the other party may be unconscious. Games are part of our unconscious and, as a result, can be difficult to understand. This section is devoted to making you aware of the many common games that are used against you. For some of these games, particular strategies to counter them are discussed. In general, however, the gaming tips listed at the end of this section will be a great help in resisting the pressures. (See the Suggested Readings at the end of this chapter for information on these and many other types of games.)

Chicken

This is a dangerous game because one party is willing to lose all in order to gain all. Although only one party is playing, both parties stand to gain or lose everything. In the game of chicken as played with cars, both drivers put their car ownership papers on the block and then speed toward each other. If one driver moves out of the way, the other gains ownership of both cars. But if neither moves out of the way, then both lose all.

In schools, a union president may threaten to call a strike unless the board of education makes a concession. He or she is playing chicken. If the board concedes the issue, the union gains all. If the board does not give in, then the union strikes and everyone loses, at least temporarily. In another example, a parent comes to her child's teacher and threatens that if he does not change the failing grade her daughter received, she will expose the number of failures, her daughter's included, that he gave. If the teacher gives in and changes the grade, then the parent gains all. If the teacher refuses, the parent faces the prospect of embarrassing her daughter by exposing her failure and of embarrassing the teacher by exposing the high number of failures he gave. Both the daughter and the teacher stand to lose.

Divide and Conquer

In this game, one party informs the other that the way to settle the dispute is simply to divide the resources. Although on the surface this may seem to be fair, in the long run it may block any process whereby the parties can explore the possibility of expanding the settlement pie. With this game, each party walks away with half of the existing pie, and neither is fully satisfied. The opportunity of creating gains that was discussed in earlier chapters is denied.

Good Guy–Bad Guy

In this game two people on one of the conflicting teams occupy different roles. One plays the tough, no-compromise, threatening role and the other plays the "we can work something out" role. The other negotiating party is caught between the tough guy who wants to seize all the gains and the nice guy who, on the surface, wants to compromise. Naturally, the attraction is to the nice guy. The negotiator works out a settlement with the nice guy influenced by fear of the tough demands coming from the other person. In this way, the apparently nice person actually is able to seize many more of the gains within the zone of acceptability than would have been possible without the tough guy's role.

Sometimes the good guy–bad guy routine backfires. The bad guy can come on too strong, making the other party feel so threatened that he or she walks out. Or the good guy may appear so convincingly able to control the tough guy that the other party feels free to offer a strong settlement package in its own favor. When the good guy then says that the package is unacceptable, the other party feels it has been betrayed by the good guy.

Nibbling

This tactic often occurs at the end of a settlement deal. Once the agreement has been hammered out, one of the parties approaches the other with a small, seemingly inconsequential request. Rather than risk the collapse of the entire settlement, which may have taken countless hours to negotiate, the other party quickly gives in. As a result, the other party gains a demand at no particular cost.

In one school district, where the principal was trying to develop an interdisciplinary team of teachers for a new program in the fall, a settlement had been reached whereby the union agreed to allow the team to work in overlapping curriculum areas. When the new program was publicly announced to an enthusiastic board of education, the union president approached the principal with a request for $5,000 to order new curriculum supplies for the program. The president said that the new program could not function without these supplies. Caught between losing his new program and publicly losing face, the principal conceded the request.

The only way to avoid this nickel-and-dime nibbling is to have the agreement contain a proposal for no add-ons. This amounts to a public statement that the settlement includes all of the items listed and nothing else.

Yes, But . . .

We have all been involved in the use of this game. No matter what you offer as a possible settlement option, the other party gives you an objection. The form may vary, but the tactic is the same. The other party wants you to reduce your settlement offer to your lowest acceptable level. In this way, it will walk away with the majority of the gains. Here is an example:

Principal: I think we can agree that the social studies and English classrooms need to be close together for this project to work.

Teacher: I agree, but perhaps in this case you should make an exception. These two rooms would need major renovations.

One way of countering this game is to offer a response that includes a "No, but . . ." You say no to the request but offer a possible consideration for the future. The other party quickly learns that you too can play a game with the same stubbornness. Responding to the teacher in the previous example, the principal might use a "no, but" approach.

Principal: I understand your request, but I do not think we can do that the first year. Let's put renovations on the agenda when we evaluate the program a year from now.

Ad Hominem

The term *ad hominem* is Latin for "to the man." It means that the game being used involves an attack on the person or persons on the other bargaining team. Rather than dealing directly with the settlement option, the other team attacks the people offering it. In this way the settlement terms are destroyed along with the credibility of the persons offering them. This game can be vicious. People can get badly hurt in the process. Those who deliver *ad hominem* attacks lack all feelings of concern about the other. They go for the jugular. This is a win–lose game from which they want to walk away with the settlement and with the other person's pride.

This game must be played in a public forum to have any value. For the attack to work, the other party needs to discredit you publicly. Most people can handle a personal attack made in the privacy of the negotiating room. But when the attack goes public it is very difficult to respond without sounding defensive, pompous, or whiny. The other party knows this and will try to misrepresent information you present, your interests, your prejudices, and your statements. Your opponent will try to get you to respond publicly to these misrepresentations. The more you play into this game, the more the other side wins. This game can sap your energy, your pride, your time, and those of your family and colleagues before it is finished. In the end you will be ready to compromise, withdraw, or concede simply to end the whole affair.

Responding to this type of game is tough. Because the attack is so personal, the stress level is very high. It is difficult to remain objective. The best advice is to consult your supporters, who can offer insights and objectivity that you have lost. They can also offer support, which you badly need. Usually, the best way to deal with this game is to remain silent. Rather than responding to each attack in piecemeal fashion, it is wise to say nothing. Bargaining needs to be postponed. Inform the other party that when the personal attacks stop, you will continue the negotiation process. Expect that your opponent will give that statement to the public in such a manner that you come across sounding defeated or guilty. But stick to your commitment and avoid any discussion of the issue outside of your support group until the game ends. And the game will end, eventually. Remember, in most cases, the other party is not out to get you personally, but is using you to get a favorable settlement. Once you refuse to play the game, it will stop, and in time the issue will lose its intensity.

Sympathy

This game also involves the manipulation of your feelings. In this case the other party tries to get you to feel guilty about the settlement option you are offering or to feel sympathy for its plight, which may or may not be related to the conflict being discussed. Although you can be empathetic and understanding of the other's plight, you need not have so much sympathy that your sense of judgment is distorted.

When the principal mentioned earlier called the teacher in to review her negative evaluation for the year, the teacher came into the office looking upset. When the principal refused to respond to the cue in her nonverbal behavior, she informed him that she had learned over the weekend that her mother needed to enter a nursing home. She spent a few more minutes explaining to the principal the complications of her situation. Whether consciously or not, she expected to elicit such sympathy from him that he would weaken his criticism of her performance.

Hardballing

Here members of the other party refuse to negotiate with you over a conflict. They prefer to let the conflict fester. Their responses may be "Let me think about it," or "There is nothing to negotiate," or even a simple "No." This game has two goals. The first is to try to get you to concede interests from the start so that you are accustomed to making concessions. The second is to allow the conflict to grow so that pressure is put on you to settle the matter in your opponent's favor.

There are various ways to influence a person who uses this tactic:

1. Complain to the other party's constituents. Tell them that you are ready to negotiate, but their leaders have refused.
2. Complain to the government or union agencies involved in the matter.
3. Make the matter a public issue by calling a press conference.
4. Inform the other party that you will delegate the issue at hand to a subordinate until the real powers on the other side are willing to talk.
5. Have the other party agree to prenegotiation talks, perhaps

among subordinates, until some meaningful issues can be brought to the table.

Johnny-Pile

When others gang up on you, you are at a disadvantage. This commonly occurs when you have to negotiate with someone who has more power than yourself. A principal going to talk with the superintendent finds herself in a meeting with the assistant superintendent, a secretary, or department directors. She is outnumbered. The others will wear you out, if not with time then with counterdemands.

The only strategy to counter this game is to take a lot of breaks. Go to the restroom, call your office, call an assistant for more information. The other team is investing more time and money in the talks than you are investing. It is costly for them to gang up on you. Wear them out. Flatter them: "Gee, I'm honored that all you important people need to help me with this issue. I know how busy you are." As the last resort, inform them that you need more time to think. If you are ganged up on, do not give in. Walk away to gain a perspective on what you are about to commit yourself to.

Table 6-3 gives you some tips on how to counter games.

MICHAEL'S CONFLICT

In Chapter Five the conflict concerning Michael's grade in English was successfully resolved. That is, all the parties involved in the conflict felt comfortable about the final settlement. During the course of the meetings the various parties directly involved did not show any overtly unpleasant or unethical behavior. The games that were played were relatively minor ones, and they did not interfere with the principal's intention to mangage the disagreement. Now, take a minute or two to look at two games that were played.

1. *Chicken:* In the initial stages of the conflict, the parents and the English teacher were playing chicken. The Jameses threatened to "expose" the teacher to the board of education. If they had followed through on this threat, they would have made everyone aware of their complaint, but they also would

TABLE 6-3. How to Counter Games

1. *Be aware:* If you are on the lookout, the game cannot be sprung on you. You will not only be expecting it but will also be prepared to counter it.

2. *Stop and think:* You need to be rational about the negotiation process. An analytical approach will help you decipher some of the processes that are occurring. Reread this section on games and try to pinpoint which ones are being used against you.

3. *Develop countering strategies:* With a little preparation, you should be able to develop tactics to bring a game to a halt. Some of those specific to each game have been discussed. In fact, if you are negotiating with someone with whom you have talked before, you will already have some idea of that person's favorite game. You should be prepared to counter it when it comes.

4. *Share feelings:* Explain how the situation affects you personally. Do not tell the other parties what they are doing but, rather, what effect they are having on you. Tell them how you feel about the negotiation so far. A statement like "I feel frustrated here" is better than "You have failed to understand the situation." Or say, "I wish we could settle this," rather than, "You are stubborn." Dealing with your feelings is harder for others than dealing with opinions or facts.

5. *If all else fails:* When the game has been sprung on you and you recognize its negative effect on the negotiation process but do not know how to get out of it, inform the other party that the game is on. Share with your opponent what you know so far about the game. Sometimes this kind of public exposure of the game is enough to bring it to an end. The other party knows that you know that the game has been discovered. Although the other party will act surprised and deny any wrongdoing, you can rest assured that the effects of the game are over. If the other side wants to continue the game or switch games, you can inform them that it is time to discontinue the game playing or you will walk out.

For further information in this area, see "Psychological Traps" by Jeffrey Z. Rubin, in *Psychology Today,* Vol. 15, 1981, pp. 69–78.

---

have made everyone aware of their son's problems in school. This public awareness could be very embarrassing to a student who has to deal with his peers and other teachers in the building.

Mr. Fritz was also playing chicken. He decided that he was going to be stubborn and refuse to have Michael transferred from his class. By leaving Michael in the class, Mr. Fritz was escalating the conflict and moving the parents closer to a confrontation with the board.

The principal was able to avoid this game by helping both parties disengage from their initial anger and their opening demands.

2. *Nibbling:* In Chapter Five we also saw how at the end of the last meeting Mr. James asks the principal for help in solving problems his son was having in social studies as well. After a long, ultimately positive negotiation process over the English grade, the father tried to transfer his success, so to speak, to another area.

The principal avoided the matter altogether by saying that the social studies problem was a separate concern, to be dealt with at a later time. He certainly did not want to link the outcome of the English grade to that of Michael's problems in social studies.

WHERE DO YOU STAND?

The best defense against dirty tricks is to have developed your own ethical standards. If you are clear in your own mind about the values you hold sacred, you will be able to rely on those values to determine how to deal with others' dirty tricks. Your values or standards will give you a fallback position when the going gets rough. You also will have no difficulty in projecting those values consistently. No matter what the other parties may do, they will get a response from you that is consistent with what you believe is right.

There are three core conditions for a viable personal ethical standard: a personal mission statement, a belief in yourself, and persistence. The way these core conditions are developed and displayed varies from person to person, but the cores remain constant. In this section each of the cores will be described. Examples of how other administrators interpret and display these cores will be provided. Finally, there will be an opportunity for you to write a brief statement of how you interpret these three conditions.

Personal Mission Statement

The personal mission statement is a vision of where you are heading rather than a list of the goals or objectives you are using to get there. For example, you may firmly believe that your school should foster the integration of the different races within your community. Your vision is one of better racial harmony and equal educational opportunity for all. This is your personal mission. The way to achieve this goal would include objectives such as heterogeneously grouped classes or teacher/staff workshops on racial sensitivity.

Your objectives may change, but your mission does not. It goes beyond satisfying your own needs. It captures your feelings about the betterment of your students, your staff, or your community. A mission statement is not something you argue about with someone else. It is a purpose that you believe in and value. You share this mission with others, but you do not open it up for debate. As one administrator put it, "It's not whether you win or lose that matters. What matters is what race you are in."

Characteristics of a mission statement include behaviors such as the following:

1. *Outcome-driven:* You have a need to see something happen as a result of your mission. You are not just satisfied to believe in it; you also want it to be fulfilled.
2. *Self-disclosure:* You proclaim your mission to everyone who works around you. If asked, your colleagues or your staff would be able to say what your vision is all about. They know this because you share it with everyone.
3. *Responsibility:* You take responsibility for your mission. It is your personal statement, so you have no need to defend it, although you will explain it to others. Whatever happens as a result of sharing this vision, it is a consequence for which you are prepared to take full responsibility.

Listed here are various mission statements displayed in different administrators' offices:

• Equal educational opportunity for all.
• If you write, you are thinking.
• A liberal education is the only education you need.
• If you measure it, it gets done.
• A safe and orderly school is the first step.
• What you nurture grows.

Activity 6-3 gives you some guidance in preparing your own mission statement.

ACTIVITY 6-3

Use this activity to prepare your own mission statement. In the spaces provided here, list some of your important beliefs.

I believe _____

I believe _____

I believe _____

     Reflect on these beliefs. Are they beliefs in different things, or can they be grouped into a broader, more general belief? Are they beliefs in attributes of yourself, in attributes of others, in principles, or in things? Can these beliefs be applied to your family life, your personal life, your career, or all of these?

     At this point rewrite each of your beliefs as a clear, concise, positive statement. This statement is one of your personal missions. Use the space provided to list your mission statements. The example shows how one elementary school principal rewrote a belief into a clear, concise, and positive mission statement.

Example: I believe *in providing an equal opportunity for all students in this building.*

Personal mission statement: All children can learn.

Your mission statements:

_____

_____

_____

_____

_____

Belief in Self

A second core condition of your ethical standard is your belief in yourself. What this means is that you give yourself positive messages, which affirm your self-worth. You see yourself as sensitive, giving, loving, concerned, competent, knowledgeable, contributing, helping, supportive, trusting, and tolerant. Your worth is determined only by you. You are the judge of how important you are to yourself. No one else can tell you that, although many people will try to do so.

Possessing self-worth does not mean that you like everything you do or fail to do. Indeed, you may have many behaviors and feelings that you wish you could change. That is the point. Your behaviors and feelings can be changed. Self-worth, however, does not depend on these factors alone. Self-worth is your own pride in yourself. It is more enduring than what you do or feel about a certain thing. People who believe in themselves have no need to talk about it. They have an internal pride that fuels their relationships with others. You do not have to convince other people that you have self-worth. If you need to do so, in fact, it is a sign that you lack self-worth.

Characteristics of a sense of self-worth are seen in such behaviors as the following:

1. *Genuineness:* You present yourself to others in a clear and consistent manner. Your personal manner is straightforward and real. There are no doubts about the fact that you believe in what you are doing because you believe in yourself. You do not seek others' approval. You do not complain because you know you can change things or at least make an honest attempt to do so.

2. *Attractiveness:* You are a positive person to be around. People are attracted to you not because of your looks but because of your beliefs. You do not seek attention or approval from others. Others do not feel that you need them to affirm your self-worth, and this makes you more attractive because you are seen not as a taker from them but rather as a giver. If you are genuine and positive about yourself, your attitude becomes contagious.

3. *Tolerance:* You do not judge people by their perceived shortcomings. You are patient with others because you are essentially at peace with yourself. You try to understand what other people believe in and what they are trying to say. You have empathy with others and do not complain about them. Instead, your approach is to try to understand people. Your view of life is one that appreciates its complexity.

Activity 6-4 is an exercise in evaluating your own belief in yourself.

Persistence

The third core condition is the quality of persistence in your attempts to make your vision a reality. This persistence means you

---

ACTIVITY 6-4

This activity will help you evaluate your own belief in yourself. After each question, circle the appropriate response, true (T) or false (F).

Can you avoid arguing about something that you believe in?   T   F

Can you say to yourself, "That is someone else's problem"?   T   F

Can you live with the fact that some people you work with will never
    understand you?   T   F

Can you allow others to disagree with you?   T   F

When you make a mistake, do you see it as a problem with your
    judgment, not with you as a person?   T   F

Do you admit to yourself that you are forever growing as a person
    and that things sometimes have to change by necessity?   T   F

Do you avoid saying, "I can't"?   T   F

    If you circled T for every one of these questions, then you can feel confident about your own sense of self-worth. You believe in yourself and are proud of what you do. If you circled F for any of the questions, go back to that question and ask it of yourself again. List examples of times when this question came up. Once you have a few examples, think of how you could have changed the way you thought, felt, or behaved about the issue. Feeling more confident about yourself may actually be the factor that will change what you do in these examples.

---

are motivated, driven, realistic, and concrete in your approach to implementing your vision. You do not give up easily.

    The other side of being persistent is being consistent. If you stick to your vision of what is important and stick to your mission of making that vision happen, then your behavior will be viewed as congruent or consistent. Your staff will not see you as a hypocrite who says one thing but allows another to happen.

    The characteristics of a persistent administrator are as follows:

    1. *Directness:* An administrator who is direct is not being aggressive or on the attack. Rather, the confrontation is based on the fact that the administrator has discovered some behavior of the other person that does not seem congruent or in harmony with that person's previous actions or words. The administrator simply points out this contradiction to the other person. This revelation to the other is based not on anger but on a true understanding of the other's behavior. The administrator's understanding or empathy has reached a level such that the administrator is sensitive to any distortions, games, or masking that occurs. The administrator directly challenges the other person to be more consistent in what he or she says and does.

2. *Immediacy:* Accomplishing your mission demands that the relationship between you and other people be direct, frank, and to the point. This ability to be immediate is rare in most people's conversations because of the underlying fear that the other person will reject you. An administrator who is immediate in his or her relations tries to help the other person understand more clearly the interests involved in the discussions. The talks therefore relate directly to what is said and done. For example, the administrator may need to tell the other party that he or she thinks a recent action is a lie, a deception, or a game. What the other party does with this direct feedback is that party's problem or responsibility, not that of the person who delivered it.

3. *Motivation:* Being able to stay focused on your vision despite all the talking, tactics, games, and interactions that are going on is a clear sign of a motivated person. During negotiations, a motivated administrator may allow the talks to move off the task of fulfilling his or her mission statement but will never let the issue fade away. He or she will find a way to let the issue resurface in another part of the negotiations. This is motivation, the fire that makes the vision a living reality in the administrator's head and heart.

Activity 6-5 will help you develop behavior that is more persistent.

SUMMARY

Although lies, deceit, and games are the dirty side of the conflict resolution process, they are also very common. You need to be vigilant in order to detect their presence and counter their influence if necessary. This chapter has concerned itself with describing how lies, deceit, and games are used by others to foster one-sided gains. Lies are common in social interactions. It is one type of lie, the self-benefit lie, that is most destructive. Three different methods of dealing with a liar were discussed. Deception is different from lying in that it distorts rather than falsifies information and is harder to

---

ACTIVITY 6-5

The goal of this exercise is to help you become more persistent in your actions. There is room here to list two actions that you would like to accomplish during this school year. These may be goals your supervisor has told you to implement, things that your staff has requested, or—most important—things you have dreamed of doing but have put off. Once you have listed the two goals, develop an action plan to get them done. If you implement these plans, or even one of them, you are demonstrating persistence.

ACTION #1

What behavior would I like to accomplish?

_____

_____

What would it look like when done?

_____

_____

With whom will I need to do it?

_____

_____

When will I start (within the next two weeks)?

_____

ACTION #2

What behavior would I like to accomplish?

_____

_____

_____

What would it look like when done?

_____

_____

_____

With whom will I need to do it?

_____

_____

When will I start (within the next two weeks)?

_____

detect. How deceivers manipulate your imagination, feelings, knowledge, and needs was discussed. Strategies were illustrated to help you unmask deceivers. Nine different games that are used to manipulate the negotiation process were described in detail. Procedures to deal with these games were presented. The last part of this chapter was devoted to facilitating an examination of your own ethical standard. The best defense against the dirty tricks of conflict resolution is to have internalized a value system based on a personal mission statement, belief in yourself, and persistence.

SUGGESTED READINGS

Acuff, Frank L., & Villere, Maurice. (1976, February). "Games Negotiators Play." *Business Horizons.*

Blanchard, Kenneth, & Peale, Norman Vincent. (1988). *The Power of Ethical Management.* New York: William Morrow.

Christie, Richard, & Geis, Florence. (1970). *Studies in Machiavellianism.* New York: Academic Press.

Dyer, Wayne. (1976). *Your Erroneous Zones.* New York: Funk & Wagnalls.

Ekman, Paul, & Friesen, Wallace V. (1974). "Detecting Deception from the Body or the Face." *Journal of Personality and Social Psychology, 29,* 288–298.

Kennedy, G. (1980). "Gambits and Tricks." In G. Kennedy, J. Benson, & J. McMillan (Eds.), *Managing Negotiations* (pp. 142–161). Englewood Cliffs, NJ: Prentice-Hall.

Lewicki, Roy L. (1983). "Lying and Deception: A Behavioral Model." In Max H. Bazerman (Ed.), *Negotiating in Organizations* (pp. 68–90). Beverly Hills, CA: Sage Publications.

Saraydar, Edward. (1984). "Modeling the Role of Conflict and Conciliation in Bargaining." *Journal of Conflict Resolution, 28,* 420–450.

CONFLICT RESOLUTION GUIDE

Each chapter in this book contains a Conflict Resolution Guide. You can use this guide as a worksheet for any ongoing conflict resolutions in which you are involved. It can serve as a checklist for determining where you are in the resolution process and where you need to go.

1. Presence of a self-beneficial lie? _____

2. Steps to deal with it:

   Ignore it _____

   Acknowledge it _____

   Confront it _____

3. Presence of deception? _____

   Do you feel doubt or uneasiness about any of your imaginings, feelings, knowledge, or needs? If so, you may be the victim of a deception.

4. Steps to deal with it:

   Unmasking the deception _____

   Changing through influence _____

   Changing through incentive _____

   Changing the ambiguity _____

   Changing the resistance _____

5. Is the negotiation going nowhere? _____

6. Steps to take:

   Ask the purpose of the meeting _____

   Listen to objections _____

   Do not argue _____

   Answer each objection _____

   Affirm your interest _____

   Move on _____

7. Are there games being played? _____

   List them here, along with a strategy to deal with each of them:

_____

_____

8. Have you developed a personal ethical standard? _____

Personal mission statement _____

Belief in yourself _____

Persistence _____

CHAPTER SEVEN

Becoming More Powerful

Power, as discussed in this book, does not mean control over people. Having power means gaining control of yourself first and then allowing others to gain control of themselves. It means that you have the authority, skills, and respect to allow others to feel that their decisions have meaning and dignity and contribute to the total welfare. This kind of power is different from what most of us have read about or been taught to seek. It is not the power to manipulate or control, but rather the power to empower others. By allowing others to take the initiative and the responsibility for resolving conflicts, the school administrator becomes more powerful.

The purpose of this chapter is to make you aware of the skills you will need in order to gain this more meaningful type of power. First, you will discover your dominant administrative style, which affects how you focus on problems and how you relate to tasks and to people. Second, you will learn to expand your style by adding skills that other administrators use. These new skills will allow you to enter conflict resolution meetings with the leadership style necessary to manage the conflict and achieve a successful resolution.

HOW YOU DISPLAY POWER

One of the foremost ways you display power is through the decision-making skills you use every day. These skills are the function of how you perceive yourself, how you react to conflict, how you deal with others, and a host of other variables. Before you can learn how to expand your power, it is necessary for you to gain some insight into how you deal with power now.

ADMINISTRATIVE STYLES

As noted in Activity 7-1, there are four different administrative styles: directive, conceptual, behavioral, and analytical. Thus the four types of administrators can be called the director, the conceptualist, the behaviorist, and the analyzer. Each of them is described here with regard to:

- Primary focus
- Job orientation
- People orientation
- Strength
- Weakness

If you are interested in more information about the interaction of job orientation and people orientation, see *Personality and Interpersonal Behavior* by Robert Bales (New York: Holt, 1970).

These styles are described only in a general manner. Read the descriptions and try to apply them to your knowledge of how you demonstrate leadership. You may need to adapt some of the descriptions to make them congruent with your self-knowledge.

The Director

This administrator can be characterized as oriented toward action, results, efficiency, and determination to complete a task.

Primary Focus

The director is oriented toward completing a goal or task. Objectives based on sound data or information are the focal point of this

━━━ ACTIVITY 7-1 ━━━

Figure 7-1, Decision Style Inventory, is based on the research of Alan J. Rowe, Ph.D., at the University of Southern California, and is used with his permission. There are many leadership style assessments available in the research. If you are interested in this type of information, refer to *SYMLOG: A System for the Multiple Level Observation of Groups* by Robert Bales (New York: The Free Press, 1979); "Jung's Theory of Psychological Types and The Myers-Briggs Type Indicator" by M. H. McCaulley, in *Advances in Psychological Assessment*, vol. 5, 1981, pp. 194, 352; and to *Personal Styles and Effective Performance* by David W. Merril and Roger H. Reid (Radnor, PA: Chilton, 1981).

The inventory used here has been supported for its reliability and validity as a test of leadership styles. For information about these statistical norms and for a more detailed description of the inventory, see *Managing with Style* by Alan J. Rowe and Richard O. Mason (San Francisco: Jossey-Bass, 1987).

This inventory contains twenty statements, each of which can be completed with one of four different responses. After reading each statement, read each of the four possible ways to complete the statement. Circle the one that best completes the statement for you.

SCORING

Once all the responses have been made, total the number of items circled in each column. Answers in column 1 represent the directive style, those in column 2 the analytical style, in column 3 the conceptual style, and in column 4 the behavioral style.

INTERPRETATION

Your scores reflect your orientation toward making decisions, or your administrative style. There are four styles: directive, conceptual, behavioral, and analytical. They are described in detail in this chapter. The column with the highest score represents the administrative style you display most of the time. It is your dominant style. The next highest score is your backup style, the behavior you adopt less frequently. If you have two or more styles with scores that are the same or within one point of each other, it means that your leadership style is flexible and diverse. You use a variety of styles at different times with great dexterity. There is no perfect style of administration. No one style is better than another. In fact, in any school building or district it is best to have a blend of all four styles represented in different personalities. This mix gives the organization the strength and flexibility to meet any crisis.

1. My prime objective is to:	Have a position with status	Be the best in my field	Achieve recognition for my work	Feel secure in my job
2. I enjoy jobs that:	Are technical and well defined	Have considerable variety	Allow independent action	Involve people
3. I expect people working for me to be:	Productive and fast	Highly capable	Committed and responsive	Receptive to suggestions
4. In my job, I look for:	Practical results	The best solutions	New approaches or ideas	Good working environment
5. I communicate best with others:	On a direct one-to-one basis	In writing	By having a group discussion	In a formal meeting
6. In my planning I emphasize:	Current problems	Meeting objectives	Future goals	Developing people's careers
7. When faced with solving a problem, I:	Rely on proven approaches	Apply careful analysis	Look for creative approaches	Rely on my feelings
8. When using information, I prefer:	Specific facts	Accurate and complete data	Broad coverage of many options	Limited data that are easily understood
9. When I am not sure about what to do, I:	Rely on intuition	Search for facts	Look for a possible compromise	Wait before making a decision
10. Whenever possible, I avoid:	Long debates	Incomplete work	Using numbers or formulas	Conflict with others
11. I am especially good at:	Remembering dates and facts	Solving difficult problems	Seeing many possibilities	Interacting with others

12. When time is important, I:	Decide and act quickly	Follow plans and priorities	Refuse to be pressured	Seek guidance or support
13. In social settings, I generally:	Speak with others	Think about what is being said	Observe what is going on	Listen to the conversation
14. I am good at remembering:	People's names	Places we met	People's faces	People's personalities
15. The work I do provides me:	The power to influence others	Challenging assignments	Achieving my personal goals	Acceptance by the group
16. I work well with those who are:	Energetic and ambitious	Self-confident	Open-minded	Polite and trusting
17. When under stress, I:	Become anxious	Concentrate on the problem	Become frustrated	Am forgetful
18. Others consider me:	Aggressive	Disciplined	Imaginative	Supportive
19. My decisions typically are:	Realistic and direct	Systematic or abstract	Broad and flexible	Sensitive to the needs of others
20. I dislike:	Losing control	Boring work	Following rules	Being rejected

Figure 7-1. Decision Style Inventory

Reprinted with permission of the author and publisher from *Managing with Style: A Guide to Understanding, Assessing, and Improving Decision Making* by Alan J. Rowe and Richard O. Mason, copyright © 1987 by Jossey-Bass Publishers, San Francisco.

style. The director will consider the data, analyze it in a general manner, and make decisions on the basis of these facts. Although the focus is on results, the director is not interested in complex long-range analysis of problems or in endless committee discussions about a matter. For a boss he or she prefers someone who is supportive but generally leaves him or her alone, a boss who states a general direction or objective and then allows enough time and personnel to complete the task. In general, these administrators enjoy the power and status that goes with their title.

Job Orientation

If you want a task completed, give it to a director. These administrators thrive on having a list of things to do and crossing off each completed item. They are apt to have daily "DO IT" lists on their desks. Directors tend to believe no one can do a job better than they can. As a result, they do many tasks they should be delegating to others.

Directors are impatient. They will involve themselves deeply in projects and will want continuous status updates on these projects. In extreme cases, they can become dictators, demanding more results from the staff. They often take risks in making decisions. In conflict resolution meetings they prefer to generate multiple options for settlement and then choose the most favorable one.

People Orientation

Directors may care less about the staff's feelings with regard to an issue than they do about results. They believe that everyone else is just as interested in completing a task as they are. Directors have a problem listening to their own feelings about issues. As a result, they have even more difficulty "hearing" the feelings of others. They tend to be dismissive about personal involvement in task completion, considering it unnecessary and even as complicating things. Rather than work with people on a task, a director would prefer to work alone. The directive administrator does not particularly like to socialize. In fact, such people may view socializing as nonproductive time—the less of it there is, the better, in their view.

Strength

The director gets things done. That is why no administrator in education can survive without some of the traits of a director. The school or the school system would gradually fall behind and lack the drive for excellence that a director provides. Directors model for others efficiency, decisiveness, and control.

Weakness

The chief weakness of directors is their lack of involvement with staff. Directors have difficulty listening and often do not seek input from others before making major decisions. They tend to have problems with handling ambiguity. Directors do not like things to remain uncompleted. They often rush to complete a task. Although the task may be finished, the outcome may not be as complete as it should be. Directors often make mistakes. They also leave loose ends, which can grow into major problems at some later date.

EXAMPLE

A principal decided after looking at the master schedule for a few weeks to make some major changes in how some of the special classes should be scheduled. Rather than offering ten-week courses in music, she decided to place music on an alternating-day schedule for a twenty-week period. This change would accommodate the problems of scheduling other courses that had to be offered for a twenty-week period. The principal announced this decision to the academic teachers but did not think of telling the music teacher about the change until the last week of school in June. The music teacher, predictably, was furious.

Teacher: You never included me in the discussions about this. This alternating-day thing makes a mess of my course.

Principal: You don't understand. There was a problem scheduling the other special courses, which meet for twenty weeks, around your course, which meets for only ten weeks. I thought I had found the perfect solution to everyone's problem by offering your course for twenty weeks but on an alternating-day schedule.

Teacher: You solved nothing! My course is ruined. I have ordered films, I have speakers and field trips planned, and now I have to change everything. You could at least have asked me my opinion.

Principal: Don't get so upset. It's only a scheduling problem.

We can undo parts of it. I'm sure there are other solutions to this problem.

Here the directive principal set out to solve a tough scheduling problem. She studied the data and made an efficient decision to move a course to alternating days. Unfortunately, she did not consider the impact this decision would have on the staff member involved. In fact, throughout this dialogue you will note her lack of sensitivity to the hurt the teacher is expressing. The director handled the strained relationship as a problem to be solved. Rather than listening to the teacher's hurt and anger, she simply informed the teacher that a new solution could be framed to meet his needs. At this point the relationship between teacher and principal needed to be addressed, not the scheduling problem.

The Conceptualist

This administrative style is characterized by a highly personable, enthusiastic approach to the job. This person relies on feelings and intuition to provide innovative solutions to problems.

Primary Focus

The conceptualist is focused on following his or her intuition or feelings about an issue. He or she reacts quickly and often dramatically to situations. The preference is to have others involved in decision making, but the conceptualist will be seen as leading the change process. Generally conceptualists are ambitious, energetic administrators who look to the future in planning. They can be visionaries in their quest for excellence. They prefer to have a boss who is also personable and shares their inspirational leadership style. They also expect the boss to recognize and reward them for their good work.

Job Orientation

Conceptualists seek innovative solutions to completing a task. They see the routine way as stodgy and uninspiring. They look at the broader issues and prefer to have everyone on the bandwagon for a particular project. This feeling of consensus meets the conceptualist's need for approval from the staff. Conceptualists are willing to give up some of their power to gain this approval. Conceptualists take risks much more often than directors do. They can handle ambiguous situations and often thrive on them. In extreme cases they are considered too dramatic and changeable. In conflict resolution meetings they prefer to apply creative settlement options that will satisfy everyone.

People Orientation

Conceptualists are people oriented. They seek approval and are the socializing force in the school. In a conceptualist's school building or district, there will always be many projects being implemented at the same time. The staff will like this type of administrator, who shows care for others' feelings and views. The conceptualist, however, rarely displays an in-depth understanding of others' problems. The positive relationships, though authentic, are usually only skin deep.

Strength

Every school or school district needs someone who can inspire and energize the staff and students. An administrator who displays a conceptualist style of leadership can make a school an exciting, pleasing, and friendly place to work. Conceptualists provide the inspiration to students and staff alike to reach for higher goals and seek higher expectations. Conceptualists complete tasks in such a manner that everyone not only knows about it but somehow feels part of it.

Weakness

Conceptualists often do not stop to check what they are doing. Driven by intuition and feelings, they sometimes lack necessary information. They will, for example, make exaggerated statements, which may or may not be valid. They are also strongly opinionated. Conceptualists have an opinion about everything and will share it with you. Because they are so close to their feelings, they can be hurt easily and are known to bear grudges if they feel slighted. They thrive on social recognition.

EXAMPLE

A conceptualist principal wanted every staff member to be part of the school's talent show. He felt that the show was an excellent way to have the staff come together and have fun. Besides, he felt, the students in the elementary school would love to see their teachers up on the stage. This is how he addressed the staff at a faculty meeting:

Principal: This is a great idea, probably the best I've heard in the fifteen years I've been here. Everyone will have fun. Even you shy ones can get on the stage for a few minutes. Come on, try it.

Teacher: You know that the night this event is being scheduled is two days before our trip to the museum. Is it possible that this is too much excitement for this time of year?

Principal: I never considered that, but actually I doubt it. A little excitement is a good thing around here. We need it.

Teacher: What do you mean by *everyone.*

Principal: All of us together—you know. Now, you wouldn't want to be left out, would you? People will be talking about this event for months afterwards.

The administrator had created what he felt was a positive, inspiring way to foster staff morale. He was quick to announce it, to make everyone welcome, and even to exaggerate its significance. He voiced his opinion about the question of too much excitement without any thought or polling of other staff members. He was convinced that everyone on the staff needed this show. He created an atmosphere of enthusiasm and outright jubilation about the event. He was moving ahead with the faculty segment of the show without even checking to see who would want to come. He just expected that everyone would be there.

The Behaviorist

Administrators with this style are known for their maximum effort to relate to others. These administrators place people before the task, are very supportive, seek stability, and are not known to initiate change.

Primary Focus

The behaviorist's focus is on relationships. How staff members relate to each other, how they feel about a program, and how supportive they need the school or school district to be are important. Because the emphasis is on the people and their feelings, the behaviorist is responsive to their needs. These administrators are seen as positive, friendly, caring leaders. Everyone speaks fondly of them and people are quick to back them if they come under criticism from a superior or from parents. Behaviorists see change as unsettling because it upsets the status quo; therefore, they believe it should be initiated only if there is minimum chance of conflict and maximum chance of full endorsement by the staff. Behaviorists prefer a boss who is similar to them in style—that is, positive, friendly, supportive, and rewarding. Power is less important to them than having approval from others.

Job Orientation

Task completion is not the highest priority of the behaviorists. They will spend hours trying to talk others into initiating change. Meetings are a common forum for planning change because behaviorists consider people's involvement the number one issue. Behavorists operate in the present, so the issue of speed in implementing a task is not crucial. In fact, behaviorists prefer to postpone a decision to change as long as possible. With regard to conflict, behaviorists would like to avoid it. In resolution meetings, they seek compromises that produce harmony.

People Orientation

Relationships are very important to behaviorists. How their staff feels is seen as the key to creating an effective school. The final decision is less important than making everyone feel part of the process. The behaviorist is not an outgoing leader. Unlike conceptualists, behaviorists would prefer to be seen as simply part of the staff of the school or the district. Whereas conceptualists can be exciting and inspiring in relating to people, behaviorists are quiet, behind-the-scenes players.

Strength

Behaviorists provide a friendly, supportive educational environment. Conflict, at least on the surface, is rare. When it does erupt, it is dealt with by trying to have the people involved work out a direct compromise. These administrators have a positive relationship with the staff and most likely socialize with staff members. For the most part, students feel comfortable in the building and view these administrators as nice people.

Weakness

Because of the primary orientation toward people, not tasks, there is the danger that change will come slowly, if at all. Behaviorists can be so concerned with staff needs that they cater to these needs. Giving in to everyone's whim allows a gridlock atmosphere to develop. Most staff members carve out little fiefdoms within which they operate, but no change can occur without interfering with these comfort zones. Discipline can be a problem if there is little administrative leadership to confront disruptive students. Some staff members view this style of leadership as being too compliant and lacking in backbone.

EXAMPLE

This principal operates with a behaviorist style. When asked by her superintendent to implement a new discipline code, she began the task by asking the staff for volunteers to work on the school improvement team. She received fifteen positive replies from teachers. To begin the meeting, she had the group meet after school. She provided a catered light snack for them. This is how she began the meeting:

Principal: Thank you all for volunteering to come to this important meeting. We need to implement a new discipline code, and this group has been given the task of developing an action plan to do it. Before we begin, make sure you all have enough food and drink. This is an informal meeting.

Teacher #1: I do not understand why we need a new code. The old one worked well.

Teacher #2: I agree. I think this new code business is an idea of the superintendent to make herself look good. There is nothing inspiring about this so-called code.

Principal: Now, I hear that you are upset. I am concerned that you two do not like the new code. Are there others who feel the same way? Perhaps we need to discuss this issue some more.

Rather than implement the new code herself, the principal called a meeting and formed a team to discuss the change. She provided a nurturing environment for the meeting. Both of these items are part of the behavorist's mode of operation. Also, when dissent developed, the principal backed away from her task and decided to discuss staff feelings. The question here is whether she can get the group back on task.

The Analyzer

The analytic administrative style is one of organization and careful planning. These administrators are task-oriented and strive for a detailed, flawless execution of change. Oriented toward thinking, these administrators are cautious and will postpone decision making until they know all the facts.

Primary Focus

Change does not come easily to analyzers. The primary reason for this is that they need to spend so much time collecting and evaluating data that the opportunity for positive change can be lost. Analyzers like routine and prefer a systematic order. They like to control things. Yet they have a high tolerance for ambiguity because they like the challenge of solving complicated tasks. Analyzers are hard workers in terms of the amount of both time and energy they devote to a task. They work well with a boss who gives them clear direction, independence, and time to evaluate a task.

Job Orientation

Analyzers like to work and like their work to be as precise as possible. If you give a job to an analyzer, you will be assured of a detailed, well-thought-out plan. Although they expend a great deal of energy to organize a task, they may also take a long time to complete it. Analyzers are not quick workers, nor do they perform well under pressure. With an analyzer, however, there will be few surprises once a plan is executed.

People Orientation

Analyzers like to work alone. Generally they are not outgoing, nor are they consensus builders. They prefer to deal with data and information rather than with people. They avoid meetings unless there is a need to collect, share, and analyze information. Group brainstorming of ideas is not their method of thinking; they prefer to think more logically and sequentially. They are respectful and obliging toward authority. They prefer to work through channels, by a person's job title, rather than referring to how a person feels about a task.

Strength

Analyzers are hard workers who get the job done and complete it well. They are industrious, persistent administrators who will look over every detail before committing themselves to action. They are opinionated only when they feel they are right. They do not seek glory for themselves and prefer a behind-the-scenes role. Their buildings and districts run smoothly and efficiently. Everyone is aware of the established rules and roles, and follows them.

Weakness

The time it takes an analyzer to complete a task is a problem. Because of their need to collect as much information as possible before committing themselves, they often do not make decisions quickly. They need time lines and should be expected to adhere strictly to deadlines. Socially, they may appear aloof and uninvolved. As building administrators, these people spend too much time dealing with paperwork such as budgets, reports, and test data, and not enough time with staff and students.

EXAMPLE

This is an exchange between an assistant superintendent and a principal over the issue of substitute teachers. The assistant superintendent displays the analytical style in her attempt to implement a new policy of dealing with substitutes.

Assistant superintendent: If you could read over these policy steps, then we can talk about them. You may have questions.

> *Principal:* I can tell you right now we have a problem. A district-wide central pooling of substitutes is going to cause us to lose control of the coverage each day.
>
> *Assistant superintendent:* Well, we spent a lot of time researching this problem of coverage. From a district point of view, by far the most efficient solution is to centralize the process. You should give it a try, because a lot of thought went into this.

This assistant superintendent had difficulty responding to the feelings of the principal. He responded to her from a cognitive rational viewpoint, thereby missing the principal's affective needs. The potential for conflict exists because of this lack of understanding of the principal's needs.

Overcoming Style Clashes

The dynamics of some of the different styles, by their very nature, have the potential to cause conflict. This is because some types of administrators view their roles as the antithesis of another's view. Although each style can conflict with any of the others, the two primary conflicts are discussed here. In these situations, both administrators have to yield a bit and respond to the other's needs in terms of implementing change.

Director and Behaviorist

The director is oriented toward completing the task. The behaviorist is oriented toward relationships among staff members. Together, these two types of administrator have the opportunity to come at a task from totally different directions. The director wants to get on with the implementation and sees the behaviorist as stalling by having too many meetings or as being too sensitive by feeling the need to respond to each staff member's criticisms. The behaviorist views the director as being too controlling and too rushed to care about the people involved in the change.

Analyzer and Conceptualist

The analyzer is not interested in the excitement and spontaneity that the conceptualist needs to thrive. Whereas the analyzer will systematically attack a problem through logical analysis, the conceptualist will look at the situation abstractly and intuitively. The analyzer will want the conceptualist to back up the ideas with data, whereas the conceptualist will want the analyzer to take a risk with an idea. The drama that the conceptualist will unfold about a problem will be an embarrassment to the analyzer, who values low-key conflict resolution meetings.

MICHAEL'S CONFLICT

It is possible to review the behavior of the principal, the teacher, the parents, and even the guidance counselor throughout this conflict settlement procedure in light of the different administrative styles displayed. Let's take a brief look at each.

The principal: This person demonstrated a director style of administration. He was primarily task-oriented; that is, he focused on resolving the conflict. He spent time gathering pertinent information as he met with the different participants. He was less interested in how the participants felt than in what they knew or thought they knew. Throughout the procedure, you as a reader do not gain much insight into how the principal was feeling. He simply did not care to share his feelings with the participants. Finally, he took control of the procedure by requesting that Mr. Fritz, the teacher, remove himself from the formal meeting. In that way the principal was able to control the interaction between the two parties.

The teacher: Mr. Fritz displayed the characteristics of a conceptualist. He was primarily feeling-oriented and demanded that his students invest as much energy in the classwork as he did in teaching. He was able to compromise and was willing to bend even his own rules. In fact, the first concession of the meeting came from the teacher. When the parents informed the principal that Michael had additional assignments in his locker that were ready to be graded, Mr. Fritz agreed to accept the work even though it was late. However, when the parents refused to turn over the work out of fear that Mr. Fritz would seek revenge and mark the papers as failures, Mr. Fritz was insulted. He responded to his feelings and wanted Michael thrown out of his class. The fact that the principal requested that Mr. Fritz be removed from the meeting may have come from a fear that the meeting could easily be reduced to an exchange of hurt feelings.

Yet without this first concession from the teacher, there is no telling how long the meeting would have gone on.

The parents: Both of the Jameses showed behavior consistent with that of analyzers. They invested considerable time and energy out of their daily schedule to deal with this matter. They were willing to wait for a positive outcome. They were task-oriented in that their chief concern was the failing grade; in fact, their initial demand was for a change in grade. In the beginning you do not hear a lot about their son's feelings. They had counted and analyzed the amount of work required of Michael and drew their conclusions from these facts. They were not at all concerned about Mr. Fritz's feelings or about the principal's feelings.

The counselor: This person showed signs of being a behaviorist. She was concerned about everyone's feelings throughout the meetings and wanted everyone to feel comfortable. Because of the tension between the teacher and the parents at the first meeting, this counselor realized that she was not prepared to handle the complex dynamics present in this conflict. She quickly sought help from the principal. Yet her concern was intense enough that she wanted to be present throughout the settlement meeting. She probably played an important role in helping the parents feel more comfortable during the meeting.

BECOMING MORE FLEXIBLE

By becoming more adept at using various administration styles, you not only become more flexible in solving conflicts, you also become more powerful. You have an increased ability to create change by allowing others to respond to your differing styles. You have different orientations to the task, to the staff, and to the presenting conflict. Looking at these factors from different angles, so to speak, allows you to develop multiple options from which you can create successful resolutions.

Listed in this section are a series of worksheets that are geared toward helping you make your dominant administrative style more flexible. Simply look for your administrative style and complete the various activities in the worksheets. You will find that these activities will help expand your flexibility and help you become a more effective and powerful administrator.

Activities for the Director

Delegation

Directors need to learn how to delegate work and projects to others. Rather than do everything themselves, they need to let others feel responsible and trusted to complete a task. Activity 7-2 will allow directors to delegate tasks without losing total control of them. The key thing to remember is: Once you delegate a task, truly let it go. Give the other person the time and resources to do it.

Listening for Feelings

Directors have difficulty responding to the affective needs of staff members. You cannot respond if you do not first *hear* those needs. In listening for feelings, try to listen for the feeling words used. In the following example, the superintendent responds to a parent's feelings by repeating back the heard feeling word.

Parent: My daughter is being picked on by these teachers. I am angry and upset. What can you do?

Superintendent: I understand that you are upset and angry.

In addition to listening for feelings, directors should use feeling words when describing projects and activities. These affective words will let your listeners know what your needs are with regard to the issues. You will be seen as a person with specific needs rather than just as a boss giving orders. For example, rather than

---

ACTIVITY 7-2

List the task to be delegated and the person to whom the task has been given. A date not too far in the future should be listed to let you monitor the person's progress.

Task	Person Responsible	Dates To Check

saying, "I would like this test evaluation done by Friday," you might say:

> *I feel uneasy about these test results. To help me understand what has happened, could you please provide me with an evaluation of the testing by Friday?*

Activity 7-3 gives you some practice in responding on the feelings level.

Activities for the Conceptualist

Getting Organized

Conceptualists need to develop additional organizational skills and incorporate these into their daily management activities. Concep-

---

ACTIVITY 7-3

Write a feeling-level response to the following comments. If no feeling word is used, try to guess what the feeling may be and use that in your response. Examples of appropriate responses are provided at the end of the activity.

1. I am disappointed in how this was done.

   Response: _____

2. I read your report and am delighted with the solution.

   Response: _____

3. Boy, what a show! Truly great.

   Response: _____

4. This program is very interesting and thorough.

   Response: _____

SOME APPROPRIATE RESPONSES

1. You feel disappointed about this.
2. You are very satisfied with this report.
3. This show really excited you.
4. You feel comfortable with this program.

tualists often make decisions on the basis of impulse or with insufficient backup data. Completing Activity 7-4 will help conceptualists organize their daily activities.

Develop Other Options

Conceptualists are people who have opinions about most things. They do not have to think about an issue for long to develop an opinion. Conceptualists do not often consider the fact that others may have different opinions. Activity 7-5 will help you develop an awareness of other opinions.

Activity for the Behaviorist

Develop Action Plans

Behavorists have difficulty making decisions under time pressure. They are often so concerned about the relationships involved in the change that the change is long in coming about. An action plan developed early in the planning can speed the process along. Activity 7-6 incorporates a specific plan, detailing who will do what and

---

ACTIVITY 7-4

Each day before you go home, take out your "DO IT" memo paper and write down three things you must do before the end of the next work day. A secretary can help you with this by providing the daily memo paper. Have your own memo paper printed. Be consistent. If things do not get done on one day, carry them over to the next. Save the memos and review them each Friday afternoon to plan for your Monday morning "DO IT" list.

DO IT

Date	Item	Done	Part Done

ACTIVITY 7-5

For each conflict resolution meeting you are about to attend, record the following information:

1. Issue to be discussed at the meeting:

   _____

   _____

2. Your opinion of the issue:

   _____

   _____

3. Two other opinions that others could hold on this issue:

   _____

   _____

   _____

4. The opinion your boss will most likely take:

   _____

   _____

   _____

when. A time line is built into the implementation. There is a column for listing how everyone will know the project is completed. Will there be a report, a verbal statement, or an activity? What will be demonstrated? Making this action plan public before the change is started forces the behaviorist to make a commitment that it will get done.

Activities for the Analyzer

Socialize

Many analyzers have difficulty exchanging small talk with others. They consider talking about family, hobbies, and their own feel-

---

ACTIVITY 7-6

Complete each section on the basis of the proposed action plan:

Activity: _____

Date of planning: _____

Purpose: _____

				Evidence of
Action Steps	*Who*	*What*	*When*	*Completion*
1. _____				_____
2. _____				_____
3. _____				_____
4. _____				_____

---

ings as unimportant. Yet others may view this small talk as a means of discovering how sensitive and human the administrator may be. Activity 7-7 will be of help to the analyzer in developing positive social relationships with others.

Hold Meetings

Analyzers tend to shun meetings. For instance, they do not like informal open faculty meetings. Yet this informal time is an opportu-

---

ACTIVITY 7-7

Obtain a list of your staff members and develop a plan to speak informally with each of them during the next week, or two weeks if the staff is large. What you talk about is less important than the fact that you do talk to them. Check off each person after you have spoken. You may want to plan to be in the school parking lot in the morning, or in the teacher's room, or in the copy room to engage the different staff members. Try to go to them rather than expecting them to come to you. Repeat this activity every few months or so.

nity for the staff to open up to the analyzer about how they feel. Analyzers can gather many good ideas if they are diligent listeners to what is being said. Activity 7-8 will help you plan a series of informal meetings with your staff. The agenda may be established or it may be open to whatever concern faculty members may have at the moment.

ACTIVITY 7-8

Complete the information for each section:

MONTHLY

Have a period of time at the end of each monthly faculty meeting to discuss any concerns.

_____

_____

ALTERNATING MONTHS

Establish open faculty meetings. Set the time and date well in advance, and inform the staff that the meeting is voluntary and open to anyone who would like to discuss any issue.

_____

_____

DEPARTMENT OR TEAM MEETINGS

Inform the chairpersons that you are going to be stopping in to hear what is going on in the meetings. Make a point of just sitting in on the meetings. You do not have to say anything. You will learn a lot and will be available if anyone has a question or comment.

_____

_____

_____

_____

THE IDEAL SCHOOL ADMINISTRATOR

Is there an ideal school administrator? The answer is an unequivocal yes! Such administrators possess all the strengths of the four different administrative styles. They are flexible in their response to dealing with day-to-day conflict on the job. They can be directors, conceptualists, behaviorists, or analyzers, depending on the skill needed to resolve the conflict. They are seen as adaptive, responsible, and competent.

They are people who, first and foremost, manage themselves well. They feel their work has purpose, meaning, and dignity. They have a vision of education that is clear and based on meaningfulness and integrity. They lead a balanced life. In one sense, they are happy and fulfilled, but they also desire continuous growth and development. They are always changing and improving themselves while holding on to their sense of self-pride and dignity. Their view of conflict is similar to their view of life. They see conflict as not necessarily negative or bad but, rather, as an opportunity to change and grow. Although they would like to avoid conflict, this positive view of the process allows them to be masters of conflict resolution.

Second, these administrators are leaders who promote power in others. They encourage others to take responsibility for themselves and for their jobs. Warren Bennis and Burt Nanus, in *Leaders: Strategies for Taking Charge* (New York: Harper & Row, 1985, p. 217), talk about the leader as one who can transform others by freeing up and pooling the collective energies of a staff in pursuit of a common goal. These are the administrators who can allow others on the staff to share in a vision of what the school or district can become. These are the administrators who reduce conflict by allowing and encouraging the staff to work together as a team to manage their own objectives and processes.

If we had to list the traits of the ideal administrator for the next decade, they would be as follows:

1. *Values:* Having a passion for fairness and compassion, well-thought-out personal values, courageous and unyielding integrity that engenders trust
2. *Vision:* Having a well-developed and articulate philosophy of what the school or district is all about
3. *Communication:* An effective listener, able to conduct a clear, concise, frequent exchange of ideas and feelings

4. *Teamwork:* Able to encourage and promote teamwork among the staff and to empower teams to make decisions and take responsibility for them
5. *Critical thinker:* Able to see problems through others' eyes and communicate this understanding; to think both logically and intuitively, to handle ambiguity, and to integrate the ideas of others
6. *Action:* Able to get things done, to lead by example and persistence, to follow up, and to accomplish things
7. *Self confidence:* Having the strength to share the credit, take risks, be patient, and maintain a sense of humor

SUMMARY

For an administrator to become more powerful, he or she does not have to learn how to take more control of events or manipulate others. Rather, administrators become powerful by allowing others to take charge of problems and assume responsibility for finding solutions. This chapter has described how this process can take place. First, the administrator needs to start with him- or herself. Assessing your own administrative style promotes self-knowledge and self-confidence. Expanding your style to include the skills of leadership characteristic of the other administrative styles is the second step to becoming more powerful. This chapter gives the reader an assessment instrument and skill development worksheets to accomplish both these tasks successfully.

REFERENCES

Bales, Robert. (1979). *SYMLOG: A System for the Multiple Level Observation of Groups.* New York: The Free Press.

Bennis, Warren, & Nanus, Burt. (1985). *Leaders: The Strategies for Taking Charge.* New York: Harper & Row.

Block, Peter. (1987). *The Empowered Manager.* San Francisco: Jossey-Bass.

Maccoby, Michael. (1988). *Why Work: Leading the New Generation.* New York: Simon & Schuster.

Merrill, David W., & Reid, Roger H. (1981). *Personal Styles and Effective Performance.* Radnor, PA: Chilton.

Rowe, Alan J., & Mason, Richard O. (1987). *Managing with Style: A Guide to Understanding, Assessing, and Improving Decision Making.* San Francisco: Jossey-Bass.

Shakeshaft, Charol. (1987). *Women in Educational Administration.* Beverly Hills, CA: Sage Publications

Vail, Peter B. (1989). *Managing as a Performing Art,* San Francisco: Jossey-Bass.

Winter, David G. (1988). "The Power Motive in Women—and Men." *Journal of Personality and Social Psychology, 54,* 510–519.

CONFLICT RESOLUTION GUIDE

In the middle of the conflict resolution process, take time to reflect on which administrative styles you are using. Also consider the other party's administrative style. Is there a potential for your style and the other's style to clash? Also, to make yourself more effective during the settlement process, you may want to consider using other administrative styles to project your views. This guide will help you in that process. Reflect on the ideas in this chapter and then choose activities from the following list that will be compatible with the orientation and strengths of the other party's administrative style. Write an activity that will support your views within the other's administrative style.

DIRECTOR

Delegate: _____

Listen for feelings: _____

CONCEPTUALIST

Get organized: _____

Develop other options: _____

BEHAVIORIST

Develop action plans: _____

ANALYZER

Socialize: _____

Hold meetings: _____

Conflict Management Revisited

To be an effective manager of conflict, you need to expand your perception of what conflict can be. If you see conflict as a dynamic process, always in a state of movement, then you can believe that this process can be intercepted and managed. Conflict need not carry only negative overtones. The processes involved in conflict can bring about a new improved order while the old is dismantled. This new order should be one that meets the needs of all the participants. Your school or school district should be a more productive and more satisfying place to work because of the settlement outcome.

To manage this conflict process, you need to learn the vocabulary of change and to work within the model offered in this book. The developer model of persuasion is used here to provide you with a conceptual process to manage change. As you will recall, this model advocates achieving change by involving all parties in disseminating information, exploring the differing interests in a dispute, and gradually building a consensus of opinion around a settlement option.

To manage conflict, you will also need to become aware of the many tactics necessary to move a dispute toward a successful settlement. In reading this book, you have learned how to set a positive climate, how to set the agenda, how to establish your best alternative to a negotiated agreement (BATNA), how to disengage from demands and anger, how to apply pressure to settle, how to find ways to settle, and how to satisfy your needs in a settlement agreement. Now you have the task of incorporating these tactics into your own work style. You will need to become skilled at using these tactics. You can do this by gradually experimenting and trying to implement the various procedures in the different conflict situations that you face. Your awareness will develop over time to a degree of competence as you successfully implement the many tactics explained in this book.

Another necessary skill in managing conflict is one that will be difficult for many busy school administrators. This is the need to take time to reflect on what is happening in a conflict situation and to listen to your own feelings. Often your intuition about an issue or a participant will give you guidance in determining what is happening during a conflict. Use these feelings as guideposts to help you implement the various skills described in this book. In addition to your own reflection on the process, you also may want to hear a close colleague's reflections on the matter. This networking of school administrators can be a powerful ally during conflict.

The final skill you need in order to become a successful manager of conflicts is to establish a personal value system, a vision of what your school or district is all about, a clear and frequent exchange of ideas among your staff, a teamwork approach to problems, an ability to handle the ambiguity of the conflict situation, and an overriding self-confidence in your ability to manage the process.

Managing conflict is work, but it can also be rewarding if you view it as a means of producing a positive change in your school or district. As a school administrator, you cannot avoid conflict. If you want to be an excellent administrator, you will need to know how to manage conflict. It is hoped that the skills in this book will assist you in your professional development toward excellence.

━━ FINAL ACTIVITY ━━

In Chapter Two, Activity 2-4 asked you to assess your skill at handling conflict. This self-measure came relatively early in the discussion of how to manage conflict. By now you have been made aware of hundreds of new skills you can use to deal successfully with conflict. Assessing yourself again will give you a self-measure of how comfortable you feel with what you have learned. Take a minute to complete this final activity and compare your rating on the scale to the rating you gave yourself on the same scale in Chapter Two.

The following scale below runs from 1 to 10, with 10 being the highest or most skilled level of conflict management. Level 5 would be considered an average level of skill. Level 1 represents no known ability to manage conflict. Where would you rate yourself? Circle the number.

10	9	8	7	6	5	4	3	2	1

Highest   Average   Low
skill level   skill level   skill level

Compare your skill level to the level you assigned yourself in Chapter Two. Did your skill level increase or decrease?

Index